D1713527

Smart Decisions

The Art of Strategic Thinking for the Decision-Making Process

Thomas N. Martin

First published 2016 by
PALGRAVE MACMILLAN

The author has asserted their right to be identified as the author of this work in accordance with the Copyright, Designs and Patents Act 1988.

Palgrave Macmillan in the UK is an imprint of Macmillan Publishers Limited, registered in England, company number 785998, of Houndmills, Basingstoke, Hampshire, RG21 6XS.

Palgrave Macmillan in the US is a division of Nature America, Inc., One New York Plaza, Suite 4500, New York, NY 10004-1562.

Palgrave Macmillan is the global academic imprint of the above companies and has companies and representatives throughout the world.

Hardback ISBN: 978–1–137–53698–3
E-PUB ISBN: 978–1–137–53699–0
E-PDF ISBN: 978–1–137–53700–3
DOI: 10.1057/9781137537003

Distribution in the UK, Europe and the rest of the world is by Palgrave Macmillan®, a division of Macmillan Publishers Limited, registered in England, company number 785998, of Houndmills, Basingstoke, Hampshire RG21 6XS.

Library of Congress Cataloging-in-Publication Data

Names: Martin, Thomas N., author.
Title: Smart decisions : the art of strategic thinking for the
    decision-making process / Thomas N. Martin.
Description: New York, NY : Palgrave Macmillan, [2015] | Includes
    bibliographical references and index.
Identifiers: LCCN 2015025954 | ISBN 9781137536983 (alk. paper)
Subjects: LCSH: Decision making. | Decision making—Case studies.
Classification: LCC HD30.23 .M3724 2015 | DDC 658.4/03—dc23 LC record
    available at http://lccn.loc.gov/2015025954

A catalogue record for the book is available from the British Library.

Printed in the United States of America.

Contents

Figures

Preface

About 18 years ago, my department chairperson asked me if I wanted to develop any new courses for our management department. I had always wondered why we did not have a course on managerial decision making since I felt it was one of the most important skills our students should have in order to become successful managers. While various personal and organizational rational programmed decision models were talked about in my other courses, this was usually only cursory classroom discussion covering a few pages in the textbooks I used. Furthermore, there was no consideration of creative decision-making processes. Thus began my journey into exploring and developing material related to creative decision-making processes that I could teach to my students so they could learn how to make better decisions in the ever-changing and uncertain world they would face in their future.

Over time and even though my course focused on managerial decision making, I learned that decision-making fundamentals could apply to more than organizational managers. A strategic decision would represent any decision that applied to something to be done in the future and that carried high value and importance for the decision maker. Deciding which wedding dress to purchase, which house to buy, which district to campaign in, or which medical treatment for cancer to pursue all represent a strategic decision for a bride, a couple, a politician, and a senior citizen, respectively.

During the years of offering this course, I have used various scholarly textbooks as well as books prepared by consultants. Doing so has provided me with the theoretical perspective to understand why the decision-making process is framed as it is and also why and where consultants have taken shortcuts in order to expedite the process. One of my major conclusions as a result of this 18-year journey is that decision makers need to modify their thinking about how they deal with acquiring and analyzing information in each of the decision-making process steps. This approach requiring thinking modification will lengthen the process, make it more complex and more arduous to some, but the comprehensiveness of the new thinking approach should lead to improved and more effective decision making. Thus, my second major conclusion is that continued shortcuts in the process in order to reach fast decisions will continue to produce the same kinds of decisions that are not well thought-out, the kind of ineffectual decisions we have seen in the past.

Key Features

The thinking required for making good, ethical decisions includes the following ten issues to be contemplated and thoughtfully dealt with by decision makers: (1) creativity is needed to produce new, innovative, but useful and feasible ideas; (2) decisions are generally about actions that are expected to take place in some future desired situation, and these actions have consequences that have to be anticipated through a future-oriented, exploratory lens; (3) decision makers will make mistakes and suffer failures, but the better, resilient, and effective decision makers learn from their mistakes and rarely make the same mistake again; (4) an ethical decision usually creates both benefits and disadvantages for different recipients of the decision; therefore, a decision cannot fully satisfy everyone; (5) the decision-making process is only as good as the information collected and properly analyzed in each step of the process; (6) numerous questions that are open-ended, thought-provoking, and deeply penetrating must be asked in each decision-making step and serve to stimulate both creative and critical thinking; (7) speed is not necessarily an ally of good, effective decision making, but having as much comprehensive, thought-provoking information as possible without suffering from information paralysis is a fundamental and necessary precondition for making good decisions; (8) even with sufficient information, decision makers often make their decisions based on their values and assumptions and intuitions, and therefore decision making is often an art, and these underlying aspects must be made transparent to others in order to foster better understandings of decisions; (9) a solution set rather than a single solution is necessary for good decision making, and this means having a primary solution and at least one or more backup or contingent solutions; finally, (10) the progression of the decision-making process leads to one and only one decision about what the ultimate solution will be, but in reality there are many separate decisions about many issues that need to be made in each step of the decision-making process, but they are all interrelated. After making these decisions, decision makers have generally completed a mental process that has required thinking about generating stimulating questions, collecting and analyzing various forms of information, executing both creative and critical thinking approaches, recognizing and making transparent their values and assumptions, accepting and learning from decision failures and mistakes, and recognizing and understanding the interconnectedness of different decisions.

Overview of the Book

The overall thinking modification framework presented in this book begins by suggesting that a decision-making process has to be uniquely applied to each of three different situational states—a current state, a future state, and, finally, a transition journey state occurring between the current and future states. Each of these situational states represents a different state of mind, both real and anticipatory, for the decision maker, and includes different physical, factual, and perceptual conditions that affect the thinking and analysis of the decision maker. For each of these three different situational states, the linear, five-step process is the same, but the underlying issues in each step are different because the three situational states themselves are different. The first step consists of a situational analysis to determine which current state conditions really need to be changed into different future state conditions. The second step focuses on identifying and framing the challenges in these situations and determining what seem to be the underlying causes. In the third step multiple options are generated and then developed into numerous solution possibilities. Deciding which of the solution alternatives will form the solution set constitutes the fourth step. The fifth and final step involves decision makers in planning how to implement the chosen solution and also in planning a set of aftermath control systems to finalize the implementation plan.

In order to comprehensively develop and investigate each of these five process steps, decision makers are asked to engage in thoroughly performing the seven thinking elements framework recommended in this book. Again, there seems to be a linear mode of conducting these seven thinking elements until feedback looping analysis is performed; then backward feedback analysis enters the decision-making process. These seven thinking elements are described more fully in the later chapters in this book. Suffice it to say here that complex and even arduous thinking is required to complete creative and critical thinking, develop evaluation criteria, and conduct feedback looping analysis and consequence analysis before arriving at the final output for each step.Various tools and techniques to create many of these thinking framework elements are also described in the following six chapters of this book. Enjoy reading about the new decision-making ideas blended with traditional ideas presented in this book and then do the hard work to think better and become a more effective decision maker.

Application to Teaching Students in Classrooms and/or Consultative Workshop Sessions

I use the material contained in this book as the basis of teaching my course Managerial Decision Making. Either individual students or student groups are required to identify initial situations they see in their work organizations that need changing, and they are then required to prepare extensive journal entries for each of the five major decision-making process steps presented in the book. The only caveat given to the students before they began this applied learning journaling approach is that they must have sources in their organization to whom they can go to get legitimate information and whom they can ask questions and get answers. After fully completing the journal, the students will have a fully developed, decision-making prospectus on what they could do to change a situation in their organization. They may then be in a good position to sell management on their decision making because of the network contacts they made in order to get the information needed for their journal entries.

Acknowledgments

For 18 years I have had the privilege of working with my students in my Management Decision Making class. They have opened my eyes and mind to the wonderful art of creative thinking as they have dealt with a myriad of different organizational situations. These students have contributed so much to deepening my understanding of what the human mind can do in improving the thinking behind making better strategic decisions. Because of the group-based journal assignment, students also learned what it takes to work together to become a high-performance team.

I want to express my thanks to all the editorial, production, and marketing people at Palgrave Macmillan for making this book what it is today. My special thanks to my editor, Laurie Harting, for all the editing of my original drafts and for providing expert improvement suggestions. My wife, Mary Ann, deserves special credit for not making special demands on my time, giving me ample opportunities to pursue writing this book, and putting up with the chaos for three years while I labored in the basement creating this book. Last, but certainly not least, I have to express my deepest and most sincere thanks to my typist, Jackie Lynch, who did such marvelous work in typing out my handwritten material and for telling me to do the thinking but leave the typing to her.

CHAPTER 1

New Thinking Directions in Decision Making

In the *60 Minutes* television broadcast on January 22, 2015, two Republican leaders in Congress talked about the kinds of high-risk, complicated decisions they will face in dealing with the president. For example, Congress will have to consider and make strategic decisions on issues such as income equality, free community college tuition, increased minimum wage, simplified tax credits, infrastructure spending and improvements, Iran sanctions and radical terrorism, and immigration reform, among many others. The police chief of Cleveland, Ohio, was interviewed in the second segment of the broadcast and asked to explain what he had done to better integrate and train his police force in order to deal with the diverse community in Cleveland. The final segment revealed the decisions a Chinese woman had made to stand up to the Chinese government and become an independent, entrepreneurial tennis star.

These are just some of the complex decisions leaders and managers face on a regular basis. Yet very few of today's decision makers have had any formal training in decision making, in determining what factors to consider, and most important, in weighing the implications and consequences of decisions.

The purpose of this book is to offer decision makers a specific thinking framework following a sequential, five-step model of the decision-making process. The thinking framework consists of seven elements that need to be clearly and specifically considered during each of the five steps of the process. Explaining the components of the five-step model of the decision-making process and the seven elements of the thinking framework will take up the major portion of this introductory chapter.

The decision-making and thinking strategies to be introduced in this book can be used by executives, managers, and others dealing with high-risk, complicated strategic decisions, such as questions of organizational resource allocations, new plant and equipment, personnel retention and reward, and/or product innovation and marketing issues. Remember, from reading the preface of this book, that strategic decisions represent any future-oriented decision that has high value and importance for the decision maker. Even parents making a decision about whether to vaccinate their children against measles or students trying to decide which college major to select or which job to take upon graduation can find the decision-making model and thinking framework presented in this book useful.

This book is based on a number of premises. The first premise is that the decision maker is also involved in the problem-solving process as well as in the decision-making process. This individual thus has two functions: first, as principal thinker in the problem-solving or opportunity-creating process, and second, as the person with the power to make and carry out decisions. The most parsimonious model incorporating critical steps from both the problem-solving and decision-making approaches is the following three-step model: (1) identify and define the problem/opportunity, (2) generate alternatives/options to handle the situation, and (3) decide on a solution and implement it.

This is not a book on how to make speedy or quick decisions. The emphasis is on collecting and thoroughly analyzing lots of information by following the five-step process of the decision-making model. The decision maker has to weigh making a hasty decision predicated on insufficient and poorly analyzed information against waiting for more information before making a decision. Proper use of the seven elements of the thinking framework in each step will allow decision makers to arrive at a decision based on fairly complete and comprehensively analyzed information.

This book is primarily for practitioners even though it is backed up with extensive scholarly research. Making decisions is both an art and a scientific endeavor. Remember that a decision represents a call to action in some future state; decisions are based on information that often consists of assumptions and can be inspirational, provisional, and anticipatory in nature. Furthermore, decision makers use their own personal values and assumptions and past experiences and/or intuitions to arrive at their decisions. All of this individualistic assessment of a situation is part of the artful approach to decision making.

Still, quite a bit of information used in decision making can be factual or based on experiments, and the investigative tools and techniques for gathering and analyzing this information are part of accepted scientific methodology. Decision makers should question the reliability and validity of the information used in the decision-making process.

There are three essential components of the model described in this book. These components are situational states, the five-step model of the decision-making process, and the seven elements of the thinking framework. These three major components are represented as the inner circle, middle circle, and outer circle, respectively, in figure 1.1.

First Component: Three Situational States

In the center of figure 1.1 is the circle labeled "three situational states." This is where the decision maker's mind is grounded in thinking about one or all three situational states. These are mental images of different situational conditions that exist in the mind of the decision maker. A current state situation would represent the mental image or state of mind of the decision maker regarding current conditions facing the decision maker. A future state situation would then represent the decision maker's mental state of mind concerning situational conditions anticipated in the future. These are two entirely different mental images existing in the mind of the decision maker and they incorporate two different thinking perspectives. A third mental thought image

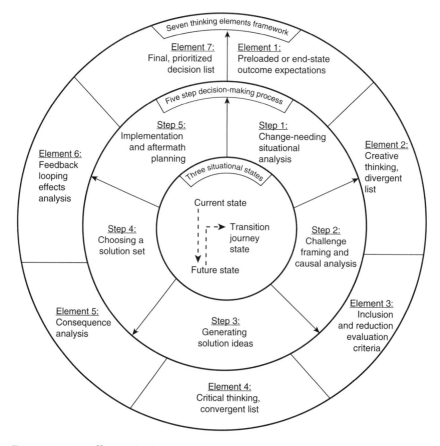

Figure 1.1 A Different Thinking Paradigm for Decision-Making Process.

occurs with the transition journey situational state, but not until later in the decision-making process. Thoughts about the what, why, when, where, who, and how regarding a current state or future state situation or a transition journey should always be on the decision maker's mind. In other words, a decision makers' fundamental responsibility is to collect and analyze information relevant to all three situational states and their interrelationships. This is essential to the potential success of the decision-making process model and the seven-element thinking framework.

A modified gap analysis shown in figure 1.2 provides the basic definitions and outlines the relationships among the three situational states. Figure 1.2 starts on the left with the decision maker's thoughts

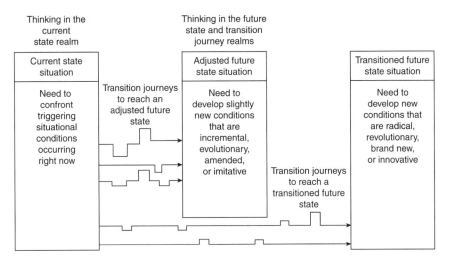

Figure 1.2 Thinking about Three Situations.

about the current state situational conditions. For example, a current state situation may represent a problem, such as the foreman of the first shift not meeting the daily performance schedule for the assembly line or a basketball coach confronting the team at halftime about being behind by 15 points. Another current state situation could also present an opportunity, such as a customer being given the opportunity to buy an upgraded insurance policy at a much lower price than originally quoted. Thus, the decision-making process begins with a current state situation that includes various conditions.

If the current conditions are deemed to require action, decision makers have to engage in thinking oriented toward a future situation. In figure 1.2, this reoriented thinking can be directed toward one or two different future states. The first future state situation is labeled the "adjusted future state"; here decision makers' thinking incrementally modifies or amends the current state conditions in an evolutionary fashion to lead to a situation that is different but still close to the original one. For example, a person in a car accident (the current state situation) would think immediately of getting out of the car and moving to a safer position (the adjusted future state). Likewise, when an employee at work has accidentally started a fire when using a blowtorch (the current state situation), the employee thinks immediately about how to put out or escape the fire (the adjusted future state situation).

The second future state situation is labeled the "transitioned future state." Here decision makers' thinking produces a future situation that is new and radically different from the original one. Many examples of current state situations being transformed into radically different future ones can easily be found. For instance, before 9/11 in 2001, airline passengers could simply walk to their airport gates and board their planes (then the current situation), but afterward the boarding procedure radically changed due to the transitioned requirements of a new government agency. Likewise, cell phones have changed the practice of telephoning with cord-connected home telephones.

The final situational analysis indicated in figure 1.2 is labeled the "transition journey" and illustrated in figure 1.2 by the lines drawn in the spaces between the current state situation and the two future state situations. This does not refer to the actual solution or decision itself but rather to the "pathway" or "route" of how a solution or decision might be realized. In figure 1.2 some of the lines are jagged as they stretch across from one situation to another to indicate that pursuing a particular transition journey might have its own set of problems or opportunities.

A rather obvious example is the Keystone Pipeline. In the beginning, the current state situation was Canada's need to get oil transported to the refineries in Texas so it could then be shipped overseas. Various future options included transporting the oil in railroad cars or through a pipeline. Consequently, one transition journey was to have various railroad companies transport the oil, and the other transition journey was to build the Keystone Pipeline. Each transition journey has produced its own set of problems. The railroad transition journey has led to crashes and dangerous fires. The Keystone Pipeline has led to court challenges from landowners as well as to efforts by Congress and the president to block the construction of the pipeline.

Consideration of transition journeys has traditionally been postponed until decision makers have made a final decision or choice and have begun implementing that particular decision; that is, this transition journey was thought about only in the last step of the decision-making process. I believe decision makers must think about what pathways or routes might be taken much earlier, namely, once potential solution options or alternatives have been developed. If serious analyses of potential problems of any transition journey are dealt with before a final solution choice is made, a different solution might be chosen. Therefore, this type of analysis should become part of the third step of the decision-making process rather than be the last step in the process.

Second Component: Five-Step Model of the Decision-Making Process

The second major component is labeled "five-step model of the decision-making process" and forms the middle circle in figure 1.1. These five process steps are to be considered sequentially. Each step requires input of information and analysis of that information through various thinking elements to reach an output in the form of answers to the major distinct decisions required to complete each step. For instance, the output information to answer the major decision to be reached in step 1 (what situations need to be changed?) then serves as the basis for generating the input information needed in step 2 (identifying the challenges in situations needing change). If the input information is faulty, insufficient, or poorly analyzed, then the step's internal conversion process will be adversely affected. The result will be faulty or inadequate output. This is one of the main reasons why intense and complex analysis of the information used in the decision-making process must be part of each of the five sequential steps of the process.

First Process Step: Change-Needing Situational Analysis

As explained regarding the first modeling component about three situational states, the decision-making process begins with identifying a variety of triggering conditions in the decision maker's current state situation. Quite often, there are many conditions and some may not be immediately obvious. The first step is to identify, clarify, and then prioritize a list of current state situational conditions the decision makers (or someone else) want changed. The need for change is usually evident when decision makers face dissatisfaction and/or other reasons that make change a necessity. The current state situational conditions represent actual or perceived objects existing in the environment or context of the situation. The decision maker has formed an impression of these conditions and this state of mind is what mentally drives or motivates the decision to change. People's basic psychological response is to move away from the dissatisfying current state condition toward a more positive future state condition. Even trying to take advantage of a current state condition that presents an opportunity expresses this movement toward change because a better, more positive future state condition is desired.

Beyond the decision maker's hopes and aspirations, there may be factual or perceived deficiencies motivating the need for change. These deficiencies could be related to timeliness, satisfying the boss or customers, handling discomfort, dealing with performance deviations or expectations for performance improvement, meeting legal or regulatory or financial and personal requirements.

Decision makers begin this process step by first identifying the current state situations possibly needing change, then acquiring additional information to clarify those situations, and finally prioritizing them. Prioritization has to occur because resource limitations constrain decision makers' ability to change all the situations previously identified and clarified.

Connecting the first process step to the previously mentioned, three situations component should be fairly obvious. The current state situation is where decision makers start: identifying what needs to be changed. Something in the initial current state situation is disruptive, triggered by either positive or negative events and/or deficiencies. This then creates motivation to think about how either a new, adjusted future state situation or a new, transitioned future state situation could result in more positive outcomes. Further clarification of either one of these new future state situations may cause additional constructive discontent that could translate into identifying even more situations needing change, now or in the future. For now, it is too early to consider thinking about transition journeys since no solutions have been proposed yet.

The distinction between the two possible future state situations—the adjusted and the transitioned one—needs further discussion. The distinction is that any adjusted future state situation is usually going to be achieved in the future by minor modifications in rules, laws, policies, and/or structural characteristics with some of the parameters of the old current state situation still left in place. A transitioned future state situation represents a highly visionary, greatly modified, and uniquely different future state situation. Thus, the anticipated degree of change desired helps determine which of the two future state situations to choose.

As an example of a negative current state situation positioned for change, consider how the Boston Marathon bombing incident affected other cities with upcoming marathons. Because many rules and policies regarding security at these events were already in place, the only changes made were to bring in more security staff and more technology to scan potential dangerous areas. This is the classic incremental adjustment methodology for most current state situations needing change and improvement. Consider what happened after 9/11 when a new, transitioned future state situation was created of having additional airport security procedures in place where there had been hardly any previously. This once new, transitioned future state situation has now become an adjusted future state situation due mainly to incremental changes, such as replacing old scanners with new total body scanners.

Second Process Step: Challenge Framing and Causal Analysis

Decision makers enter the second process step with a list of current state situations needing change and the relevant anticipated future state situations. This step has two main phases. In the first phase, decision makers perform an analysis of the crucial factors that supposedly created the need to change the current state situation. At the same time, they must also identify the crucial underlying factors in the corresponding future state situation that might prevent its realization.

Both sets of factors (hereafter called "challenges") must be identified, clarified, and finally prioritized. Crucial current state challenges must be understood so they do not appear in the future situations, or if they do appear there, decision makers will have gained information after completing this step on how to deal with those future challenges. The second phase of the step is the analysis of the underlying causes of the challenges in both situational states.

The ultimate emphasis in the remaining decision-making steps will be on dealing with those challenges that carry crucial possibilities of deterring the eventual successful realization of the new future state situations. These challenges are normally tagged as problem-related challenges. They are generally perceived as future factors that will produce negative disturbance, discrepancy, or perceptions that something is wrong. Not doing something about them may eventually cause the realization of the future state situation to be unsuccessful. The other generally perceived challenges are opportunity-related challenges; they are perceived as needing resolution in the future because attaining a solution provides even more positive potential benefit in the future.

In addition to problem- and opportunity-related challenges, other challenges could arise from other sources. Not attaining designated goals, objectives, and/or end-state key performance outcomes or not reducing the deficiencies previously noted could also be viewed as serious challenges.

Having completed the first phase of this step, the second phase, causal analysis, begins after the lists of both serious and potentially persistent current state challenges as well as vitally critical future state challenges have been prioritized. Here decision makers should strenuously engage in trying to identify, clarify, and prioritize the underlying causes of the crucial challenges being advanced into the future state situations.

The basic premise is that unless the underlying true rather than merely symptomatic causes of the challenges can be identified, the eventual solutions applied to overcome these challenges will not result in the desired future state. The decision maker will have done these things if true causes aren't dealt with! Decision makers will have wasted time and resources because without dealing with the underlying true causes of the challenges, solutions will be applied only to symptoms rather than causes, and this increases the risk of failure occurring in the future state situation.

This relationship is demonstrated in the following formula:

Causes → Symptoms → Problem → Options → Solution → Consequences

Many times, decision makers develop a solution directed at dealing only with the symptoms of a situation. This symptomatic solution approach is performed because doing a real causal analysis is too costly or too time-consuming or may prevent making a quick decision. If the solution does eliminate or reduce the symptoms of a problem, decision makers are still left with the equation:

Causes → ~~Symptoms~~ → Problems → Options → Solutions → Consequences

This still means the problem will continue to exist because its true causes were never addressed.

Third Process Step: Generating Solution Ideas

In this third process step, decision makers should have a list of crucial future state challenges and a possible indication of their causes. Normally, this is viewed as the step requiring the greatest amount of creative thinking because generating all kinds of options or alternative ideas is pursued first before utilizing criteria to develop these ideas into potential solutions. The thinking protocol in this step requires multitasking and follows a different thinking sequence than was followed in the previous two steps.

The thinking protocol sequence in the previous two steps was identification, definitional clarification, and prioritization. In this step, the thinking protocol sequence changes to generation, further development, and prioritization.

The multitask nature and complexity of thinking in this step is developed in two ways. First, decision makers must be able to utilize two sets of criteria depending upon whether options and/or alternative ideas are being generated or potential solutions are being developed. A second layer of thinking complexity is added depending on how a potential solution should be related to the type of challenge (problem or opportunity). Should a potential solution be reducing or enhancing a particular challenge?

As previously mentioned, generating options or alternative ideas to deal with the future state's challenges and their underlying causes is the first requirement for creative thinking here. Assessing these ideas is where creative criteria are needed and generally these criteria must be new and innovative. Options or alternatives are considered to be preliminary or tentative and could be ideas that are visionary, whacky, practical, controversial, conventional, impossible, innovative, unafford-able, combinational, borrowed from other disciplines, dream-related, radical change-related, incremental change-related, or any other ideas that could be transformed through further thinking.[1] Unless decision makers push themselves or are pushed by others to be creative, there is a strong tendency to revert to making modifications to existing, nor-mal, obvious, rational, and familiar ideas.

Once the requirement of creative thinking is imposed to generate new ideas, these ideas must then be developed into potential, use-able solutions, and a different set of criteria is used for this activity. A second set of business- or reality-related criteria, namely, reasonable-ness, feasibility, and practicality (usefulness) now becomes dominant. Unfortunately, these criteria will allow personal experience and intui-tion along with old, conventional ideas related to incremental change and/or ideas that have been worked before, to enter the thinking arena. In the end, any surviving developed solutions should be developed sufficiently to meet most of the criteria of newness, reasonableness, feasibility, and practicality (usefulness). The requirement that the final solution list must contain at least some new and innovative ideas is important because these challenges are located in new future state situ-ations in which old solutions probably do not apply.

Finally, being cognizant of the relationship between the type of chal-lenge (problem or opportunity) and its potential solution adds to the complexity of thinking in this process step. If the concern is with generating potential solutions regarding problem-related challenges, then these solutions ought to focus on how to reduce, neutralize, or eliminate those challenges and their causes. If the concern is about opportunity-related challenges, then the focus would generally be on ideas for enhancing, or strengthening those challenges and their causes. In the end, any new and innovative solution ideas must be developed enough to be considered practical or useful.

Consider how these two criteria would affect decisions in the following example. Moviegoers and TV watchers of *Star Trek* are familiar with the phrase "Beam me up, Scotty" and have long been fascinated by the transporter mechanism. Clearly, if a person had to travel between New York and Los Angeles, using such a transporter beam would be a new and innovative transportation solution, but is it practical and useful given the state of technology and resources we now have?

Fourth Process Step: Choosing a Solution Set

Essentially, this is the process step in which the solution is finally chosen that is assumed to successfully handle the previously identified challenges of the future state situation and their causes. Traditionally, criteria (hereafter called "solution success criteria") would now be applied to the potential solutions developed in the previous step and the result would now be a chosen, single solution. This step then essentially has three major activities. In the first activity, a list of solution success criteria is created or made available, in the second activity, the solution success criteria are applied against potential solution ideas to make the final choice and in the third major activity, preliminary monitoring, learning, and sustainability, solution-only control systems are created. A decision process is needed to determine the solution success criteria, and a separate decision process is needed to make the final solution decision.

The way solution success criteria have been traditionally developed can bias the process and decision makers against being creative. Moreover, it may be shortsighted to choose only one solution. A final shortcoming of this traditional process step is an apparent lack of developing preliminary solution control systems.

In the first activity of this step, decision makers wait until the last possible moment to identify the list of solution success criteria. This step consists in bringing together designated conditions that impose requirements any chosen solution must meet together with a list of everything decision makers want that particular solution to accomplish in order for the future state situation to be deemed successful. Essentially, solution success criteria define what the solution must achieve to be successful at handling the challenges in the new future state situation and their causes and at preventing earlier current state situational challenges from recurring.

Waiting to focus on creating the solution success criteria is based on a desire to minimize biasing the generation of solution ideas in the previous process step, minimize biasing the identification of challenges in the second step, and overall minimize biasing the use of naïve creative thinking in any of the process steps. A number of predetermined outcome expectations determined by management could essentially set boundaries for solutions and could bias the creative generation of solution ideas in the previous step.

It was deemed necessary in the previous process step to include some new and innovative solution ideas. Therefore, it seems feasible to locate the final solution success criteria list as close to making the selection decision as possible and certainly only after solution ideas have been generated. This should help reduce, but will not entirely eliminate, bias in making a solution choice.

The second activity of this process step consists of generating and developing an actual solution set of choices rather than determining a single solution. Determining the solution set is usually an exercise in applying various quantitative tools and techniques to analytically make a decision. A solution set contains a primary solution and one or two backup solutions. While it would seem logical to have only one solution set, there may be situations in which multiple solution sets would be prudent, and then these multiple solution sets have to be prioritized.

After choices for a solution set have been made, there may be a variety of criteria to now prioritize the different solutions (primary and backup). Four criteria seem to be primary, and these four criteria could also have been used to prioritize the previously identified solution success criteria. These criteria question whether the *timeline* for a particular solution is realistic and feasible, whether the *resources* are available to get solution outcomes successfully implemented, whether available *intelligence and information* are sufficient to successfully meet or exceed the risks of solution failure, and whether the proposed solution *consequences* create more benefits than harm.

If these four criteria are used as primary, prioritization-based criteria, they are used after decisions about solution success criteria and solution set choices have been made. It is also possible that these four criteria could be used as initial assessment-based criteria for ranking solution success criteria or for choosing the rank ordering of the solutions in a solution set. For example, meeting a definite timeline and/or not encountering certain negative, detrimental consequences could be part of the required original success criteria for a solution. Alternatively, a solution set could be chosen because all the solutions in the set had available resources in a time frame that seemed to ensure positive results. The decision makers must prioritize which of the apparently successful solutions will be the primary solution and which will be the first and second backup solutions. Use of these four criterion and their prioritization could help make these decisions.

The completion of the third activity of this step centers on establishing three solution-based control systems. While a complete control system would require four formal steps to be completed, only the first two formal steps of identifying baseline goals/objectives or standards and assigning measurement metrics to them can be completed at this time. The three solution-based control systems are (1) a monitoring system focusing on the solution to check whether the designated goals/objectives/standards the solution is meant to handle are indeed being met, (2) a learning control system focusing on identifying mistakes, errors, and/or failures in the solution and ways to deal with them preliminarily, and (3) a sustainability control system that would analyze information to see whether a successful solution is sustainable in the long term. The remaining two formal control steps needed for a full control system will be worked on in the next process step, but since a solution has been identified in this process step, it is prudent to set up a preliminary control system for the solution while it is still fresh in the mind of the decision makers.

Fifth Process Step: Implementation and Aftermath Planning

This last process step would seem pretty simple to perform. Decision makers have a solution before beginning this step and must formulate an implementation plan for that solution. However, a complete implementation plan would normally be split into "pre-implementation," "during implementation," and "post-implementation" phases. If decision makers do not stay committed to completing all three phases and to developing an overall control system covering all three phases, then this last process step and the overall decision-making process could result in failure.

Unfortunately, a number of shortcuts in this step can increase the risk of failure. For example, some members of executive management may feel they have used their environmental scanning resources to identify situations needing change (step 1), used their extensive and abundant information channels to define challenges and solution ideas (steps 2 and 3), and used their power and control over organizational resources to evaluate and decide on a solution (step 4). It is then time to delegate this last step to employees with more technical, operational, and project management expertise. Consequently, the real decision makers who fully understood all the information up to the moment of putting any decision into practice have now left the scene, and the operational people assigned to do the implementation work are given only minimal guidance regarding budgets and outcome expectations.

In addition, the concept of "aftermath planning" requires further thinking as to what happens after completing the original implementation plan. The original implementation plan normally covers only the actions to be taken during the before and during implementation phases. This plan is approved and monitoring control systems are created to ensure that it is carried out. However, the people responsible for executing the plan often forget that implementation of innovative solutions is subject to mistakes and usually does not proceed without a hitch. Therefore, implementation-based learning control systems should be developed, something that is usually not done, unfortunately.

It is critical to extend monitoring and learning control systems for post-implementation plans. Finally, the three preliminary solution-based control systems from the previous step must now be reexamined.

This would entail thinking through the four necessary formal parts needed for any complete control system.[2] The first part is to identify the baseline goals/objectives or standards of the entity being controlled. Next comes identifying and developing measurement metrics to see whether the entity is accomplishing the established goals, objectives, or standards. The third part requires comparing actual performance against the expected performance standards to determine whether the entity is in control. The final part, if needed, is to take corrective action by analyzing the causes of not being in control and correcting any deviations from standards in order to get realigned to achieve the intended goals, objectives, or standards.

Thinking required to establish an implementation plan in its entirety has generally followed four sequential stages. These stages are identified as follows:[3]

Stage 1: Generate action steps

Stage 2: Aggregate resources

Stage 3: Align resources

Stage 4: Determine plan outcomes

Generating action steps (stage 1) means identifying each task needed to implement the chosen solution. Aggregating resources (stage 2) requires careful and diligent identification of all physical and human resources needed to perform the implementation and solution. Aligning resources (stage 3) means imposing formal responsibility/

accountability connections between the people needed to perform specific tasks. Finally, determining plan outcomes (stage 4) identifies and assigns measurable outcomes to be achieved for each action step.

If the process concludes without fully addressing the activities in the post-implementation phase, then all the parties involved in this decision-making process will not know whether the implementation plan was successfully carried out or ran into problems; they will also not know whether the solutions implemented successfully met the intended goals, objectives, or standards for which they were designed. Furthermore, management would not know then whether the new solution was sustained well after implementation. Providing appropriate thinking and consideration of the operational outcome of the solution and its separate implementation plan and control systems constitutes the whole post-implementation, aftermath planning and evaluation. Leaving this phase out would be analogous to a person going to the racetrack, reviewing all the horses, selecting one to place a bet on, sitting in the stands, and watching the race, but leaving at just the time one of the horses crosses the finish line and is declared the winner. Decision makers should follow up and know whether the decision-making work had a successful outcome or resulted in failure. Therefore, it would seem reasonable that additional resources be extended beyond pre-implementation and during implementation planning into post-implementation planning so as to complete implementation planning.

Third Component: Seven Thinking Elements Framework

The above descriptions of the five-step decision-making process explain the types and foci of the thinking energies required of decision makers to execute the overall decision-making process. What remains to be explained is how this thinking format might be carried out. This will focus attention on the third major thinking component labeled "seven thinking elements framework" displayed as the outer ring of figure 1.1.

The specifics on how these seven elements will be used in each of the five major steps of the decision-making process will be discussed in each of the succeeding chapters. For now, a brief overview of each element will be presented. Most books on the decision-making process provide very good descriptions of the activities to perform in each step, the tools and techniques used, and illustrations of examples using the various tools and techniques. There is, however, little insight as to the key questions, significant information gathering areas, and other thinking protocol issues that might lead to more prudent decision making. Clearly, what is being presented here with this seven thinking elements framework represents only one type of many possible thinking paradigms, but it's one of the first presented in detail.

In fact, the display of these seven thinking elements might take one of two alternative pats. The most likely path, illustrated as path A in figure 1.3, would seem to support more creative thinking than path B.

As shown in figure 1.3, the only difference between path A and path B is the placement of the inclusionary evaluation criteria. This type of evaluation criteria identifies what items, issues, or ideas must be retained

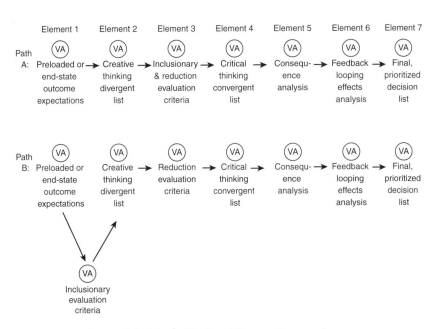

Figure 1.3 Paths A and B of Seven Thinking Elements Framework.

as the thinking framework progresses. In path A, the inclusionary criteria are placed with other evaluation criteria labeled "reduction evaluation criteria" to form element 3. These two evaluation criteria are placed
between the divergent list (element 2) and the convergent list (element
4). In path B, the inclusionary criteria immediately follow the identity
of predetermined goals, objectives, or end-state outcome expectations
(element 1) and then are acting alone to influence the establishment of
the divergent list. If decision makers want to maximize creative thinking within the divergent list, then path A offers greater opportunity
to do so. The symbol VA represents the decision makers' values and
assumptions used to decide the outcome of each element.

Thinking Element 1: Preloaded or End-State Outcome Expectations

The ultimate aim of the decision-making process is to arrive at a
solution that will handle the future challenges that need to be dealt
with if the situation needing to be changed is going to be changed
successfully.

Decision making, like all motivated human behavior, is directed at
satisfying or achieving some kind of target or outcome. In all five steps
of the decision-making process there is a central decision focus, and
decisions must be made about each step's central focus. The decision
foci include identifying the situations needing change in step 1, challenges and subsequent causes in step 2, potential solutions in step 3,
solution success criteria and a chosen solution set in step 4 together
with three solution-only control systems, and an implementation plan
and attendant aftermath control systems in step 5. Decision makers
need initial guidance and targets or expected performance outcomes
for each of these major decision foci. While specific targets can be
identified for each of the main foci in the five process steps, the main
set of targets is determined based on what is needed to attain the ultimate future situation and is usually preordained by management.
Determining the specifics of this first element serves to guide the other
six thinking elements to their respective conclusions.

Thinking Element 2: Creative Thinking Divergent List

Even though the first thinking element of locating specific preloaded goals, objectives, or designated performance outcome expectations might limit creative thinking to some degree, creative thinking is given more opportunity to blossom in this second element. The purpose of this element is to generate many, varied, and unusual ideas about the issue involved in the specific process step. Consequently, the divergent list ought to go beyond containing the old, conventional ideas that are usually delivered in the first attempt at creative thinking. There are a number of personal characteristics necessary for this type of thinking to occur: (1) fluency, in which a large number of ideas are generated (aiming for quantity rather than quality); (2) flexibility, in which different varieties or categories of ideas are generated; (3) elaboration, in which refinements or extensions of ideas occur; (4) originality, in which new or different ideas are created; (5) postponement of judging or evaluating ideas; and (6) freewheeling and combining of ideas in order to foster uniqueness and originality.[4]

Remember that decision makers go through a thinking protocol of identification first, then clarification in which decision makers are asked what additional information beyond the general information needs to be gathered and analyzed, and finally, prioritizing of the ideas based on their usefulness. The notion of prioritizing on the basis of usefulness may seem contrary to the desired nonjudgmental, freewheeling approach previously recommended, but prioritizing comes after these desired creative thinking features are subsumed into the two thinking protocol activities of identification and clarification. One might even make the case that determining the usefulness of ideas can lend itself to creative thinking.

Thinking Element 3: Inclusionary and Reduction Evaluation Criteria

There is a vital gap not covered in the traditional literature on decision making, namely, the gap between how a varied, expansive divergent list gets reduced to a much shorter convergent list. Clearly, some type of evaluation scheme has been used between the expansive listing and the reduction listing.

The evaluation criteria to help decide which ideas are retained are labeled "inclusionary evaluation criteria" and the criteria used to eliminate ideas are labeled "reduction evaluation criteria." These two sets of criteria are not merely opposites of each other. In other words, decision makers are not advised to devise a comprehensive inclusionary evaluation criteria list and then simply reverse that to obtain the reduction evaluation criteria. In some instances, creating mere opposites of one list may be appropriate, but creating distinctly different criteria would be more beneficial.

Clearly, the previously defined critical preloaded goals, objectives, or designated end state or performance outcome expectations from element 1 would have to be considered prime inclusionary criteria. For example, if executive managers indicate that they would not fund any new product ideas unless they could show 18 percent return on investment (ROI), then any proposal exceeding 18 percent ROI should be included for further funding consideration. The 18 percent ROI preloaded objective would therefore become an inclusionary evaluation criterion.

Other explicit, formal and previously predetermined inclusionary evaluation criteria might emerge from analyzing information dealing with regulation and/or organizational rules and policies, laws, standard operating procedures, customer requirements, ethical decision-making practices, national benchmarking standards, or any other requirements imposed by superiors and/or external conditions. All these criteria would constitute the general category of environmental, organizational, or contextual evaluation criteria. Depending on whether a particular criterion exceeds or falls below the stated requirements, that criterion could be considered inclusionary or belonging on the reduction list. The previous example of setting an ROI at 18 percent was fairly obvious: a proposal would make the cut at or above 18 percent but would probably be excluded at less than 18 percent (thus becoming a reduction evaluation criterion). However, there may be other redeeming features of a proposal allowing it to advance to the next evaluation stage. This example illustrates the problem previously mentioned about merely reversing the score on one criterion to then get its opposite.

In addition to explicit, formal criteria, there are implicit, informal evaluation criteria. The principal source of these criteria could be the personal and idiosyncratic nature of the decision makers' intuition or personal ambitions, personal biases or prejudices, values, and desired behaviors. Inclusion of these types of personal criteria introduces the notion of politics into the thinking of decision making. Playing politics is part of decision making, but this topic is beyond the scope of this book.

Assume that all the previously mentioned criteria come from known sources such that decision makers have to do little thinking about developing these evaluation criteria. However, if the desire is to push and expand the limits of creative thinking, then the criteria to evaluate these new frontiers must also undergo creative cognitive development. This means that foresight, anticipatory, provisional, and inspirational thinking must enter the development of evaluation criteria alongside known formal and/or informal criteria. However, decision makers must make sure that any creative criteria can be backed up with substantial informed speculation.

The two major categories of informal personal and formal environmental, organizational, and contextual evaluation criteria come together to create the range of evaluation criteria to be analyzed in that particular step of the process. There is no set number or limitation on the number of criteria, but the widest possible range of pertinent criteria should be used. Remember that decision makers are cautioned against simply turning one type of criterion into its opposite to obtain the other type; instead, they are encouraged to identify specific criteria of each type (inclusionary and reduction) and for each of the two major categories of personal and environmental/ organizational and other contextual criteria. This way there are two distinctive and visible lights illuminating the decision makers' evaluation scheme.

Thinking Element 4: Critical Thinking Convergent List

Applying the evaluation criteria to the divergent list results in a shorter convergent list. Decision makers need to try to still modify those ideas in this convergent list. These modifications could occur as a result of implementing the 5 Rs approach as part of the remaining elements in the thinking framework once the initial convergent list has been established.

The 5 Rs are identified as reanalysis, redevelopment, refinement, resortment, and reprioritization. This thinking scrutiny will be revisited on each item in the initial convergent list as additional information comes from the fifth and sixth elements in the framework. How this occurs is explained in the next element.

Like divergent thinkers, convergent thinkers are asked to follow certain principles to guide their critical thinking. The first principle is "affirmative judgment," which is to assert that ideas have both positive and negative attributes. Therefore, decision makers are asked to avoid focusing exclusively on shortcomings and limitations and not immediately eliminate the idea. Instead, decision makers should look for the positive attributes in an idea and see whether that idea can be refined, combined, or expanded for more usefulness. The second principle is to "keep novelty alive." It suggests that decision makers should not jettison new and novel ideas developed in the divergent list simply because they are new and as yet untried. The third principle is to "check your objectives"; this suggests that the convergent list ideas chosen initially must be realistic contenders to fit the reality of the situation. The result of following the second and third principles is that novel ideas are produced that are ultimately useful and successful in meeting the needs of different stakeholders. The fourth and final principle is to "stay focused on investing the necessary energy and thought to ensure that the best ideas, not the most expedient ideas, are being developed and then selected."[5] This convergent list should contain ideas that have real initial merit to handle the decision foci the process step is trying to deal with, and some new and novel ideas should be included along with conventional ideas that will be subject to continuous application of the 5 R's approach.

Thinking Element 5: Consequence Analysis

The notion of incurring consequences stipulates that every decision made will produce consequences. Consequences are different from goals, objectives, or desired outcomes developed in the first thinking element. The latter represents what the decision is expected to achieve at some future time, but the former (consequences) refers to the aftermath of a decision put into action, now or projected for the future. Normally, and at a minimum, the classification of consequences should reflect actual (indicative of current action) types of positive and negative consequences and perceived (indicative of visualized future action) types of positive and negative consequences.

Further distinctions of actual and perceived consequences could be made for long-term and short-term consequences, physical and social consequences, and direct and indirect consequences.[6] Notice that the analysis always involves pairs of consequences: positive and negative, short-term and long-term, for example. The caution taken for analyzing long-term and short-term consequences is that decision makers often make short-term decisions for quick fixes that then can explode into producing long-term harmful consequences. Therefore, if a definite timeline is important, then decision makers should distinguish between long-term and short-term consequences. Physical consequences are often measured in terms of costs or savings. However, social consequences in terms of stress, dissatisfaction, or resistance or to a decision are not as apparent as physical consequences. Decisions have consequences for the social patterns of people's behaviors and for their interactions with one another. Sometimes a decision produces consequences directly for the situation at hand, but there may be secondary or indirect consequences occurring long after the direct consequences. Becoming aware of these indirect consequences may be one of the important deciding factors in making the decision.

In the past, consequence analyses were not usually conducted until a solution had been chosen, which usually occurs in step 4 of the decision-making process. However, critical decisions are to be made in each decision-making step and that step's decision will have consequences for decisions in subsequent steps since the decision-making process is sequential. Consequently, some form of a consequence analysis needs to be performed on each item on the convergent list.

The initial main form of the consequence analysis will be labeled as an "as is consequence analysis." To conduct an "as is" analysis, decision makers assume for each item on the convergent list that it will be put into action in its original state and will produce consequences. The major positive and negative consequences (assumed already in action) and/or major perceived positive and negative consequences (assumed to result from future action) are then identified. The other types or categories of consequences identified may also be included in the analysis.

There is an additional form of consequence analysis labeled "failure-related consequence analysis" that has particular relevance to just solutions. Since solutions are not dealt with until steps 3, 4, and 5 of the decision-making process, this form of consequence analysis does not join the "as is consequence analysis" until the decision makers work on those three steps. Leadership Professor Thomas Harvey and his colleagues suggest that there are two types of failure-related consequences.[7] One type is caused by the negative impact of the failure of a solution's implementation plan; this impact can affect both the decision makers and/or their organization. A second type of failure-related consequence considers the negative consequences caused if the solution itself fails. Providing a failure consequence analysis of either a potential solution or the chosen solution together with analysis of how any solution implementation plans could fail constitutes a much more detailed and serious analysis. Both of these types of failure consequences could produce a large cash drain for the organization and/or take a major psychological toll on the personnel and other decision stakeholders.

Decision makers have been asked to perform a preliminary failure-related consequence analysis beginning in process step 3 (generate solution ideas) even before a final solution set will be chosen in step 4 and before implementation plans will be developed in the final process step 5 (where performing the failure-related, solution implementation consequence analysis becomes relevant). Clearly, this puts the decision makers' thinking at the extremes of future-oriented, anticipatory, and provisional thinking. The purpose of performing this highly speculative thinking regarding possible failure of a solution is to cause decision makers to pause before further pursuing that particular solution in process step 3 and to reanalyze, redevelop, or refine that idea for a potential solution.

While it could be argued that each of these two types of yet-to-be failure-related consequences could be simply added to the original negative "as is consequence analysis," it might be prudent to collect more feedback information and keep them as two separate types of consequences. This might allow decision makers to assign probability estimates to the importance of the following three categories of negative consequences: (1) negative "as is" consequences, (2) consequences of solution implementation plan failure, and (3) consequences of solution failure.

Immediately following any consequence analysis item, decision makers are then required to determine a decision rule so that a realistic assessment of benefits and costs of an action and its consequences can be appraised. Decision makers try to further develop the convergent list of ideas through the continual use of the 5 Rs approach (reanalysis, redevelopment, refinement, re-sortment, and reprioritization) into more realistic and useful ideas. This developmental push toward more realism and usefulness can be achieved in one of three ways as determined by three different decision rules. The first decision rule maximizes the benefits of the major positive consequences of an item on the convergent list. The second decision rule minimizes the costs of the major negative consequences. The third decision rule pursues some combination of maximizing the benefits of the most attractive positive consequence and at the same time tries to minimize the costs of the most harmful negative consequences. Clearly, only the major positive and negative consequences would have to be determined already because it is only the highly beneficiary and/or highly devastating consequences that are used to decide which decision rule to follow.

The decision rule outcome can also be used as a surrogate decision result. A maximizing decision rule outcome essentially conveys that the decision has produced either real or anticipated positive results, whereas a minimization rule essentially conveys a lot of real or anticipated negative results have been produced, and decision makers are trying to reduce them. The combination decision rule suggests that the results of that particular decision need further analysis and refinement. The implied distinctions between these different decision rule outcomes of the consequence analysis will become even more important in the next thinking element of feedback looping effects analysis.

Thinking Element 6: Feedback Looping Effects Analysis

In traditional decision models, the subject of this thinking element has not been made transparent. This thinking framework element deals with an analysis format for evaluating different types of feedback information. That serious efforts have been lacking seems strangely odd since generating, obtaining, and analyzing all kinds of feedback information is at the core of prudent decision making. In fact, the ability to apply the five previously mentioned thinking elements heavily depends on the feedback information already generated, collected, and/or analyzed.

There are many facets to adequately performing a feedback looping effects analysis. First, decision makers have to perform backward feedback looping. In the process of performing this type of analysis, decision makers have to decide whether to conduct single-loop, double-loop, or triple-loop analyses.

Backward feedback looping means that decision makers have to loop back through all previously gathered feedback information and the sources used in the previous five thinking elements of that particular process step and may even need to revisit the information and its sources in earlier steps of the decision-making process. For example, while working in the third step of the decision-making process on generating potential solution ideas and after arriving at a preliminary list of potential solution ideas, decision makers may suspect that these

solutions do not seem to successfully address the challenges identified in the previous step of the process. Decision makers are then
faced with having to loop back through the current process step's
five thinking elements and the challenge framing and causal analysis
dealt with in the previous process step. As a result of this, the decision makers may conclude that the original challenges and/or causes
developed in the preceding step of the process were not well thought
out and must be reexamined. The feedback looping effects analysis
occurred in a backward manner and included reanalyzing the feedback information obtained in the analysis in a previous step of the
process.

Backward looping allows decision makers to apply rational, analytical thinking to past feedback information. However, the analysis of
the information derived in the thinking elements framework beyond
the first preloaded or expected outcomes element requires the exercise of foresight, provisional, and inspirational thinking. This type and
style of proactive, anticipatory thinking is vital in applying most of
the thinking elements in any of the five steps of the decision-making
process.

To explain how single-loop, double-loop, and triple-loop feedback
works, a basic feedback model is presented in figure 1.4.

The sequential nature of thinking presented in figure 1.4 indicates
that the decision maker acquires feedback information from four different sources.[8] The respective analyses of three types of single-, double-,
and triple-loop effects are also illustrated.

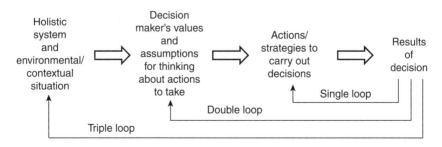

Figure 1.4   Feedback Looping Modeling Components.

Rational decision makers begin feedback analysis by generating and analyzing information about the holistic and environmental/contextual situation. The feedback information from the analysis of the holistic system suggests that a decision is needed to do something about the situation. Asked to begin developing a decision, the personal values and assumptions of the decision makers feed additional information into the process of making that decision. The decision made will necessarily specify actions or strategies that people will be required to implement. Ultimately, the decision makers and others want to acquire feedback information about the results of the decision.

The single-loop sequence begins with the decision result at the far right side of figure 1.4. The decision result could be assumed to be faulty or questionable and then loops back to the question of whether the actions or strategies decided on were correct or faulty. A double-loop sequence again starts out with assumed faulty decision results but then loops back to reanalysis of all the decision makers' values and assumptions used to arrive at the decision. A triple-loop sequence again begins with a faulty decision result, but it has to loop back to question the wider and more comprehensive initial situation the decision makers faced.

The factual information about a decision's actual result could only come from the monitoring control systems in the post-implementation or last step of the process. This would be too late a point for conducting analyses of feedback looping effects. Therefore, a substitute decision result has to be assessed. This substitute decision result is the decision rule from the consequence analysis. Figure 1.5 indicates the connection between the decision rule derived from consequence analysis and the three looping effects in the seven thinking elements framework after the decision rule is assessed.

Performing a single-loop feedback looping analysis requires decision makers to reanalyze, redevelop, refine, re-sort, and/or reprioritize the original items on the convergent list since these are the proposed action or strategy-related items. Decision makers would have started the single-loop feedback analysis focusing on the consequence analysis of the decision rule for that decision action. For example, if the decision rule was to minimize negative consequences, decision makers would

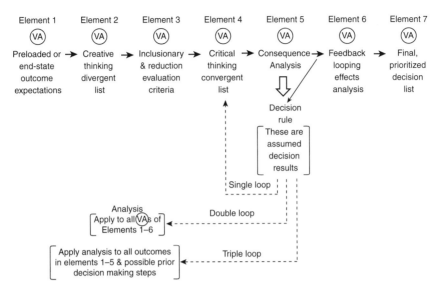

Figure 1.5 Backward Feedback Looping Effects Analysis.

have to loop back to the original convergent list items and consider a better choice, or in the absence of better choices, they would have to begin using the 5 Rs approach on that particular item in order to reduce, neutralize, or convert the major negative consequences of that decision.

Performing a double-loop feedback analysis would again start with the decision rule provided by the consequence analysis and then require the decision makers to loop back through all the VA symbols indicated in figure 1.5. Essentially, double-loop feedback is rethinking the original underlying values and assumptions that were used by the decision makers and perhaps making them more transparent and explicit to the decision makers and to those who will be affected by the decision.

A triple-loop feedback analysis also starts with the consequence analysis of the decision rule and then scrutinizes only the outputs of each of the prior five thinking elements in that particular step of the process. Furthermore, the triple-loop analysis may require the decision makers to reanalyze the respective decision action outcomes and thinking framework elements of previous steps in the process.

Irrespective of whether the decision rule suggests maximizing positive consequences, minimizing negative consequences, or making a decision to do both, feedback looping effects analysis must be conducted. Obviously, a decision rule to maximize implies accentuating the positive consequences and the decision makers may perhaps have to do only little feedback looping. However, when the decision rule is to concentrate on minimizing negative consequences, much more feedback looping analysis is required, especially if the generative affirmation principle is to be followed. The combinational decision rule would also suggest that some emphasis must be placed on feedback looping analysis, especially on reconsidering what produced the major positive consequences. Then these consequences could be strengthened, and those producing the major negative consequences could be reduced, neutralized, or eliminated.

In the end, there is a unique relationship between consequence analysis (element 5) and feedback looping effects analysis (element 6). Making a decision carries consequences not only for the decision makers but also for other people affected by the decision. The decision makers must think through what the consequences of their decision might be in the short term as well as in the long term; they must collect and analyze more and varied forms of feedback information in order to be better informed for projecting what consequences might occur and the potential impact their decisions might have. That is, decision makers must be transparent and explicit about the values, assumptions, and reasons that were part of the decision-making process. Serious, diligent, and prudent decision making requires decision makers to move away from making quick, short-term decisions toward utilizing the 5 Rs approach (reanalysis, redevelopment, refinement, re-sortment, and reprioritization) in an extended process focused on feedback and intense thinking.

Thinking Element 7: Final, Prioritized Decision List

At last, the decision makers have reached the final element of the thinking framework. This final list will contain only those items relevant to the central decision foci in that particular step of the decision-making process. For example, in the second process step dealing with challenge framing and causal analysis, the seventh and final thinking element would contain only those challenges and their underlying causes that are deemed most important to move on to the next step in the process.

The decision makers, having diligently processed the previous six thinking elements, now have a list of decision outcomes that should help to successfully complete the requirement of that particular step in the process. This list should include many vital ideas, some of which are new and innovative as well as some that are old, conventional, and slightly modified for improvement; all the ideas on the list are reasonable, feasible, and useful.

Now comes the final requirement imposed on this list by the thinking-element framework. Because most decision makers and their organizations are limited with respect to time and human and physical resources, all the decision outcomes on this final list probably cannot be executed and/or there may be certain decision that are more easily executed than others, and therefore a prioritized list is required. This prioritization process is usually accomplished with the use of various tools and techniques befitting the specific step in the decision-making process and will be identified in the succeeding chapters.

Summary

The new decision-making paradigm presented here extends the traditional model of the decision-making process with a number of new analyses and thinking improvements in an effort to make the whole process of making better decisions more transparent and explicit. This book presents a modified five-step traditional model of the decision-making process and explains a thinking framework composed of seven thinking elements to be used in each of the five process steps. Further details and specifics of how this modified decision-making model and this thinking framework are blended will be demonstrated in succeeding chapters.

Among some of the new thinking improvements are the following: (1) expanding the notion of problems into the realm of considering problems, opportunities, and other issues requiring decisions now being labeled "challenges"; (2) making more explicit and transparent the need to determine formally the two different types of evaluation criteria (inclusionary and reduction) that are needed to reduce the large, expansive divergent list into the smaller convergent list; (3) utilizing consequence analyses in all five steps of the decision-making process rather than only in the final two steps and also highlighting the need to conclude each consequence analysis with a decision rule; (4) requiring a thorough and comprehensive feedback looping effects analysis, whether single-loop, double-loop, or triple-loop feedback analyses, in each step of the decision-making process; and (5) requiring continuous application of the 5 Rs approach (reanalyze, redevelop, refine, re-sort, and reprioritize) in all remaining thinking elements after a convergent list has been established.

Decision making in today's complex, dynamic, and uncertain world requires a new decision-making paradigm and shift in thinking. The approach recommended in this book attempts to make the decision-making process more transparent and explicit so decision makers gain a real understanding of the hard, lengthy, and arduous mental work required to make prudent, well-considered, and successful decisions. This is not a quick process. In fact, the initial reaction of many decision makers upon seeing all the work required as presented in figure 1.1 might be to flee the decision-making scene because a quick calculation of fully completing all five process steps and the seven thinking elements for each step across all three different situational states would require thinking through 105 separate mental episodes.

Obviously, there is a difference in the degree of in-depth mental analysis, development, and arduous, hard thinking required. In many instances, information is already available from known sources, and the decision makers have to do little additional thinking about generating or analyzing additional information. Real intense cognitive development and analysis is required when creative thinking and serious insightful and anticipatory thinking are required.

As a society, we rely perhaps too much on computer technology, efficient information retrieval systems, sophisticated analytical tools and techniques, and continuous benchmarking and advances to the exclusion of using our brain capacity to think. Consequently, we have not produced well-considered, successful decisions about the challenges we face. Returning to the human intellect to be able to think things out rather than hoping that technology will provide the answers for our decision making is the underlying theme of this book. Let's begin the journey to increase our human thinking capacity to make better decisions in the next chapter.

Seven Thinking Elements Framework Completion Box

The thinking framework in this book might appear to be complicated – and it can be so. But once you begin to understand and utilize the framework more frequently, you will see that this methodology will become easier to use. The following completion box offers a thinking-questioning methodology for using the seven thinking elements presented at the end of this chapter. The box identifies the sequence of the seven framework elements and poses a central question decision makers might want to ask in order to effectively use that particular thinking element. Each of the five steps of the decision-making process has major decisions that need to be made in order for the process step to be successfully completed. The seven thinking elements of the framework are to be used in each of the five steps of the process. While the seven elements questions are generalized, they must be directly tied to the process step's major decision in order to be helpful in that particular process step. The decision makers would therefore use a particular element-related question to begin thinking about and collecting and analyzing information germane to that particular framework element used in that specific step of the process.

In succeeding chapters, there is a different kind of completion box in each. The succeeding chapters specifically focus on each of the five steps of the decision-making process. The decision makers are asked to address questions relative to what thoughts, ideas, and actions might be needed in order to identify the major decisions that must be made to successfully complete that process step. Therefore, this chapter's completion box is the only place where questions for dealing with the seven thinking elements framework are presented.

Element 1: Preloaded or End-State Outcome Expectations

Question: Do you, as the decision maker, have a realistic and fairly comprehensive understanding of what current strategic goals/objectives and/or key end-state operational performance outcomes were not achieved and what future ones should now be achieved?

You need to answer this basic question because answers to this question focus the rest of the thinking framework elements. Answers serve as "beacons" or "targets" on what and why a particular process step issue needs to be changed. Without answers to this question, any future decision and subsequent actions will have little direction and merit, and strategies needed to execute a decision will probably flounder.

Element 2: Creative Thinking Divergent List

Question: Has a large quantity of different ideas or thoughts been presented that will lead to new and different future situational results and is there basic understanding among all contributors of these ideas or thoughts?

Creative thinking is needed to pursue this element, and a large quantity of ideas or thoughts must be supported. The quality of the ideas or thoughts is not paramount in this element. However, clarity in understanding each idea or thought is needed so that different ideas or thoughts could be "piggybacked" into more creative ones.

Element 3: Inclusionary and Reduction Evaluation Criteria

Question: Have the vital evaluation criteria needed to reach the preloaded and/or end-state outcome expectations (element 1) as well as those from all the parties involved in handling the particular process step's major decision been carefully considered and utilized?

Not all the previously generated, ideas or thoughts on the divergent list can be utilized, so some form of evaluation criteria must be identified to either retain or eliminate some of these ideas from further consideration. It is especially important to see that inclusionary criteria are not simply the reverse of reduction criteria, but instead each type is uniquely different the other.

Element 4: Critical Thinking, Convergent List

Question: What creative (new and different), future-oriented ideas or thoughts now seem reasonable, feasible, and useful as ways to achieve the major decisions to be made in the particular process step?

After applying the evaluation criteria (element 3) against the creative divergent list (element 2), the decision makers are left with new ideas that are considered conditional until later framework elements and additional thinking protocols have been applied. These are preliminary ideas that should have real legitimacy regarding the major decisions to be arrived at in that particular process step.

Element 5: Consequence Analysis

Question: If adopted right now as is, will the specific conditional idea or thought (element #4) attain the preloaded or end-state outcome expectations (element 1) and/or satisfy the major decisions reached in the particular process step or could further improvement still be obtained with more feedback information and developmental thinking?

Still in a future-oriented thinking manner, the decision makers now must address the consequences any of the ideas on the convergent list could produce as if they were adopted. Because of the decision rule that must be determined, there is a continuous push to improve the development of that idea. It is imperative that the decision makers realistically evaluate the axiom that every decision has consequences, and prudent decision makers try to maximize beneficial consequences.

Element 6: Feedback Looping Effects Analysis

Question: Are you, as a decision maker, fairly comfortable with analyzing the information you currently have or do you suspect that you need to have more information about any particular previous process step or thinking framework element, and if so, where should you perform additional informational analysis, and where do you require more information?

A broad sweep of thinking is needed in this element. Thinking here is not necessarily focused on the need to acquire more information, but it is focused more on possibly reviewing the information already collected and reanalyzing projected important information as suggested by performing different feedback looping options.

Element 7: Final, Prioritized Decision List

Question: Have you, as the decision maker, diligently and comprehensively thought through all the possible issues related to this particular process step's major decisions and are you fairly confident that all or most of the parties to the process step's decisions support those decisions?

With this last thinking framework element, the decision makers should feel fairly comfortable with handling this particular process step's major decisions. Since this process is designed for making a decision that will be utilized in a future situation, there will still be some degree of uncertainty and anxiety about the future. The decision makers need to make the decision and get it implemented; not making a decision will probably perpetuate the frustration and problems of the current situation.

CHAPTER 2

Current, Future, and Transition Journey Situational Analysis

Let's suppose that you are the director of a stage play in its first rehearsal. Before the rehearsal begins, you have met with the three principal actors and perceived that one of them had not rehearsed his lines very well; he kept asking where the script reader was and if this person would be close by to feed him lines. You also had a conversation with the lighting director who told you that that a bank of lights was out. The lighting director was hopeful that the lights would be ready when needed a third of the way through rehearsal. The sound manager let you know that she had not yet been able to secure a device to produce an important sound for the play. As you entered the auditorium, the producer approached and indicates the performance was already over budget by $20,000.

You are now seated in the second row of the auditorium and yelling "Action!" The light gets brighter, and there's activity on the stage. You see two of the three principal actors on stage, but where is the third actor? Shortly, the third actor runs onto the stage and almost trips over a rug that should have been placed somewhere else. Everyone gasps, but the action continues. Given the potential rug tripping hazard, all three actors have their backs to you, and you can hardly hear them. Suddenly, there is a loud voice, your voice, in the theater yelling "Cut!" Many discussions now take place about how things need to be done differently in the next rehearsal. As director, you now have to decide which situations need your attention.

Like this director, executives, managers, scientists, engineers, politicians, school administrators, and even parents face similar current, messy situational conditions they want changed into something less messy or more beneficial in a future situation. They all recognize that past decisions and solutions along with the original pathways of carrying out those decisions may not work in future situations. This example reveals the central concepts of this chapter.

The director faces a number of messy current state situational conditions, among them an actor who apparently seems unprepared (a perceived condition), a lighting director failing to have all the necessary lights ready (an actual condition), a sound manager not having the necessary equipment to produce a critical sound (an actual condition), a producer who is concerned about running over budget (an actual condition), a stage manager placing a prop incorrectly (could be an actual or perceived condition depending on what the script designated), and the onstage, first rehearsal being a catastrophe (an actual condition). At this point, the director's thinking might be cluttered with conditional issues, such as why are these people not doing their jobs, what to do about these situational conditions, which conditions clearly need to be rectified now, which can wait, and what would improved conditions in the next rehearsal look like? Furthermore, the director may be thinking about the pathways (called transition journeys) needed to convert the messy, current state conditions into improved, beneficial future state conditions.

The director needs other thinking and analysis aspects. The seven thinking elements framework previewed in the previous chapter is to be applied in the current and the future state situational analyses. Both situational analyses include three new terms: identification, clarification, and prioritization. These represent three sequential protocols for information gathering and analysis. Throughout the five-step decision-making process, a different three-phase thinking protocol will be applied; remember that it has a specific sequence and is different from the seven thinking elements framework.

The identification protocol in this process step is used to gather preliminary information on situational conditions and to gain a basic understanding of which conditions might need to be changed. The clarification protocol digs deeper into situational information to provide greater understanding of the conditions identified as triggering the need for change. Making comparisons with other assessment conditions and criteria is vital at this stage. The prioritization protocol is an assessment arrangement in which the various triggering conditions, as well as the situations themselves, are rank ordered.

Situational conditions are states of affairs, events, or combinations of physical, mental, or behaviorally described circumstances actually or perceptually occurring in a situation. These events or circumstances could relate to environmental, economic, production, physical, resource, or personnel factors or any other factors.

As previously explained in the example, the director is dealing with more actual conditions than perceived conditions in the current state situations. Having more actual conditions than perceived conditions would be common for most current state situational analysis. The thinking necessary for analyzing future state situations will generally have to be highly visionary, anticipatory, proactive, conjectural, inspirational, or simply focused on what is desired on the part of the decision makers. However, this future state situation has to have some degree of relationship to the original messy situation because the future situation is a replacement of the current situation with the messiness alleviated.

If decision makers aim at taking action so as to reach an improved future state situation, then why spend so much time and effort investigating the messy, current state situation? Unless the triggering conditions in the current situation are understood, they could creep into the adjusted future state, which usually is an incrementally improved version of the messy current state situation. Alternatively, the conditions requiring change could also creep into a supposedly brand new, transitioned future state situation because anything new has some reference to past conditions. The underlying objective of both an adjusted and a transitional, future state analysis is to continue the critical thinking process of identification and clarification and strengthening the legitimacy claims of the situation initially chosen, as requiring change.

An additional preliminary thinking recommendation offered to decision makers and particularly relevant for the director's evaluation of the first rehearsal described above is presented by William Altier, a management consultant. He points out that decision makers should dissect and recast seemingly unsolvable messes into manageable, small, discrete segments or pieces rather than combining several supposedly related pieces into one big catchall messy situation. This caution is provided for two reasons. First, combining everything into one big catchall situation is assumed to make the situation easier to solve, but the conclusions reached about the larger situation could be weak or wrong. Second, the responsibility and accountability for solving complex large problem situations are hard to assign to any one person, but dividing the situation into discrete smaller pieces makes problem solving traceable, mistakes can be traced more easily to their source, and accountability and responsibility now become more transparent.[1]

Current State Situational Analysis and Identification and Clarification Protocols

Identifying the current state situational conditions starts the process of problem solving and decision making. This means gathering information to understand what is going on. Decision makers must find out what conditions in the current situation cause concern or require change, whether these triggering conditions relate to the personal feelings or self-interest of the decision makers and/or the environmental and cultural context of the organization.

Tim Hurson, a management consultant, suggests that a messy situation creates discomfort or dissatisfaction for the person concerned, who is then motivated to want to change that situation.[2] Jerry Harvey, writing about the Abilene paradox,[3] indicates that group-related triggering conditions may arise because of differences or conflicts in the personal needs, attitudes, biases, skills, knowledge, and constraints of each group member.

Triggering conditions related to an organization may include its culture mission, strategies, managerial hierarchy, decision-making processes; they may also be related to the company's interactions with its supply chain partners, competitors, regulators, and to its social responsibilities. Messiness in the context of a business organization is mainly due to inefficient and ineffective use of its resources (people, money, facilities, and time) resulting in not meeting its strategic goals/objectives or its end-state key performance outcomes, which are often considered absolute, inviolable, or preordained. Situational messiness could also come about because critical necessities such as not meeting time requirements, boss or customer demands, legal or regulatory requirements, continuous improvement requirements, or employee demands are not being met. End-state key performance outcomes are actions that operational units in the organization must routinely and ultimately achieve if the latter is to function properly. Examples of these performance outcomes of operational units could include a hospital providing patient services, a paper mill producing rolls of paper, an accounting department preparing paychecks and billing customers, a call center answering customer inquiries, or a high-tech electronics firm designing its products better than its competitors. These actions represent operational performance goals or objectives to be performed in an ongoing fashion in core capabilities, key customer segments, employee growth and development areas, and the overall organizational culture and governance structure.

Strategic goals and objectives are different from expected operational performance outcomes, and they signify what the organization intends to pursue in the future. Strategic objectives relate to the organization's competitive advantage, future products and markets, capabilities needed to provide those future products and services; that is, strategic objectives relate to long-term growth and financial targets the company wants to achieve.

Not achieving either the strategic objectives or the functional performance outcomes can trigger a sense that something must be changed in the future. For example, if management's strategic objective is to capture 20 percent of the market for a new computer model in the next six months, but after three months the organization still has captured only 8 percent of the market, there may be cause for concern. Suppose this same computer manufacturer had found its only supplier of hard drives incurred a 50 percent in-house, inspection rejection rate that shut down its assembly line 50 percent of the time over the past week resulting in underproducing the number of new computers by 100 units. Do both of these situations warrant being called messy?

The interesting thing about both situations is that each provided feedback information. What would have to happen if no real-time feedback information was provided and how would this affect management's decision making? Answers to these questions will be revealed later in the chapter and in succeeding chapters.

A major triggering event used in business-related decision making, according to the literature produced by numerous professors and consultants, is whether a problem or an opportunity is causing the messiness.[4] Diagnosing a problem or identifying an opportunity is central to the decision-making process, and how to make this identification will be shown in the next chapter. A problem or predicament signifies that there is a need to fix something that is broken and represents a difficult, complicated, or perplexing challenge that affects the situational conditions. In contrast, an opportunity signifies that a more favorable situation can be created in the future, but that situation is not part of the current situation.[5] The initial identification protocol produces a list of current state triggering conditions that now need to be further clarified and better understood.

Chris Grivas, an organizational and leadership consultant, and Gerald Puccio, a professor and management consultant, indicate that clarification of a situation means sorting out the underlying real items from the symptoms or distractions, looking at the relevant data, measuring all aspects of the situation, asking probing questions, working to understand the history of the situation, and assembling as complete a picture of the situation as possible.[6] Some of these data are readily available, but other data are implicit, anticipatory, and provisional. Specific data sources include feedback information, feelings, observations, impressions, guesses, hypotheses, and gaps in information.[7]

The focus of the thinking protocol should be on clarifying that part of the situation where improvement and change will have the greatest impact. Without this investment of time to clarify the current situation needing change, improvement efforts will be scattered, inefficient, and ultimately wasteful.

Managers have to be internal and external environmental analysts as they try to align resources with strategic goals and objectives or achieve end state, key operational performance outcomes. Tony Proctor, an emeritus professor of marketing whose book on problem solving is now in its fourth edition, indicates that decision makers can identify and clarify their respective improvement and change-oriented situations in several ways: first, by comparing current experiences with others; second, by comparing current experiences with current strategic objectives or plans; third, by comparing current performance with models of desirable and/or benchmarked key, operational performance outcomes; and fourth, by comparing current performance with that of other organizations (competitors, suppliers, customer organizations) or some of their own subunit operations.[8]

Current State Situational Analysis and Seven Thinking Elements Framework

In chapter 1, the seven thinking elements framework was described. This step is the first opportunity to see these seven different thinking elements in action. The first four elements—identification of the predetermined strategic goals and objectives and/or end-state, key performance outcome expectations, creation of the divergent list, determination of inclusionary and reduction evaluation criteria, and creation of a convergent list—are the most important elements for conducting an analysis of the current state situation. Although all seven elements might be used in a specific current state situational analysis, most decision makers find it appropriate to end their analysis with the creation of the convergent list of the most relevant current state situations needing change. Thinking can then turn to situational analysis of the future state situation.

In using thinking element 1 decision makers first need to know what the strategic goals and objectives and/or end- state key performance outcomes are and which ones are not being met. Without this information comparing the current state situation to these targets, the decision-making process may be problematic. Thinking element 1 essentially establishes a strategy and a boundary condition for a goal that must be achieved by taking action.

Various situations that have conditions involved in not accomplishing thinking element 1 would be items placed on the divergent list. This lengthy list is then subjected to evaluation criteria that eliminate or retain various current situations. Finally, since the reduced convergent list may still remain somewhat messy and ill-defined, further clarification must be applied to those remaining current situations on the list. This may result in further refinement, reprioritization, and even in different situational choices. Various tools are available for carrying out the above-mentioned four thinking framework elements.

The most useful tool for identifying the situational conditions is to ask questions. William Altier provides a list of starting questions, including neutral, information-gathering questions as well as questions about value judgments:[9]

Neutral	Value-Based
What uncertainties, unknowns exist?	What is bothering you?
What questions need to be addressed?	What concerns do you have?
What is going differently than expected?	What is not meeting expectations?
What is not guaranteed, is not a sure thing?	What is exceeding expectations?
What moves could someone else make that could change things?	What could be going better?

Tim Hurson concentrates on asking the following questions to tap emotional reactions and personal views and idiosyncratic views of worth such as:[10]

What's bugging you?	What would you like to see different?
What's out of balance?	What challenges are you facing?
What needs to be resolved?	What do you wish worked better?
What could be improved?	If your itch was a t-shirt slogan, what would it say?
What would you like to change?	

He continues his "ask questions—collect information" approach by asking his main trigger condition question, "What's the itch?" He then proceeds to ask three more questions and gather more information: "What's the impact of the itch?" (what effect does the itch have and why is it important?); "What's the information surrounding the itch?" (what is known about the itch, its causes, and what else might need to be known about the itch?); and finally, "Who's involved relative to the itch?" (who are the stakeholders, who might be affected by the itch, and who might or is influencing the itch?).

Scott Isaksen, Brian Doval, and Donald Treffinger, acclaimed authors and professors, recommend the following word checklists as a way to stretch people's imagination about possible triggering conditions in a current situation:[11]

- What would you like to...

correct?	improve?
change?	do away with?
turn around?	convince others?
resolve?	produce?
eliminate?	humanize?

- Are there opportunities for...

programs?	procedures?
production?	plans?
public impact?	services?
policies?	laws?

Current State Situational Analysis and Evaluation Criteria

The change-needing current state situation needs to be converted into a new future state situation, and this need for change can be triggered by three general factors: psychological, environmental, and personal factors. Psychological factors include discontent, desire for better conditions, or simply a desire for change. Environmental factors include demands from management, from clients/customers, or from the organization, usually in regard to objectives not being met. Finally, personal factors include egotistical desires or personal deficits that are not currently being met.

Now it is time to look at what tools/techniques can be used to create the evaluation criteria that will be used to reduce or retain the previously generated list of potential messy current state situations needing change. Use of evaluation criteria could also subtly begin the prioritization protocol.

Evaluation criteria can come from a variety of sources, for example, from the strategic goals/objectives and end-state key performance outcomes identified in the first thinking framework element. The decision makers or management could have designated some of these objectives as "must" objectives and others as "want" objectives. The "must" category means that the objectives definitely must be achieved, and if they cannot be achieved, the situation is listed as one needing change.

The "want" category of objectives means that decision makers would like to see these objectives realized and will rank them in some way. Depending on the ranking of these objectives, the evaluated situation may or may not be one that needs change. For example, a committee of senior executives for the evaluation of new projects could issue a declaration that any new proposals "must" have an ROI of 18 percent and that they "want" proposals mainly in the areas of personnel development and new technology.

Much of the information for evaluation criteria can be assessed with a very simple tool called I^3, which stands for influence, importance, and imagination.[12] These three criteria are related to the personal characteristics and preferences people bring to their task of judging the most relevant current situations needing change.

Influence is the ability to take action and can be assessed regarding its strength with the help of questions such as: "Do you feel you have enough clout or leverage to effect the change needed in the situation?" "Do you or the decision making group have the authority or responsibility for implementing the results or outcomes of your work on changing a situation?"[13] Decision makers must distinguish between influence and control because even when they do not have complete control over a situation, decision makers may have a high degree of influence.[14]

Importance or interest refers to the degree to which decision makers care about changing the situation and therefore want to deal with it. This factor represents the degree of emotional and motivational investment in pursuing the task of changing the current situation. The essential question here is: "Do you really want to work on this challenge, or are you indifferent or negative about this task?"[15]

Imagination refers to the decision makers' need for novelty, new directions, possibilities, ideas, solutions, or actions. The essential question here is: "Do you wish or need to consider something new?" And if the answer is yes, then this need will motivate people to engage in creative thinking to produce novel ideas.[16]

Using this tool simply involves creating a matrix like the one shown in figure 2.1. Adding up the number of checks across a matrix row

Influence	Importance	Imagination	Brief current situation description or evaluation criteria
	√		Situation 1 (eval. criterion 1)
√	√	√	Situation 2 (eval. criterion 2)
√	√		Situation 3 (eval. criterion 3)
√	√	√	Situation 4 (eval. criterion 4)

Figure 2.1   Illustration of I³ Evaluation Technique.

reveals that situations 2 and 4 are relatively the most important. Remember that this tool could also be used to prioritize evaluation criteria by replacing the description of the current situation with the evaluation criteria.

The final thinking element in dealing with the analysis of the current situation is usually determining the situations with the most messy current conditions that then becomes candidates for the convergent list. Many tools are available for developing the convergent list of current situations. Jay Couger and Tony Proctor, both professors and management consultants, provide an extensive number of tools, some of which have already been described.[17] These tools include SWOT analysis, 5 Ws/H or interrogatives, laddering and progressive abstraction, goal/wish orientation, boundary examination, why/why method, decomposable matrices, cause-and-effect or Fishbone diagrams, lotus blossom method, and disjointed incrementalism.

The lotus blossom technique illustrated in figure 2.2 involves peeling back the petals around the core of the blossom one at a time.

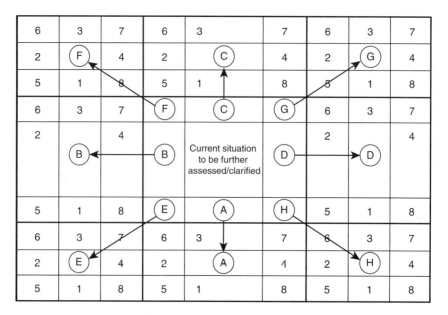

Figure 2.2   Usage Format of Lotus Blossom Technique.

Decision makers could begin by placing a short description of the current situation in the middle of the matrix and then writing various triggering conditions associated with that current situation in each of the boxes lettered A through H. Then each of the component ideas in A through H can be further fleshed out until a messy situation is comprehensively clarified. Notice that each cell allows for eight ideas to be identified.[18]

Disjointed incrementalism is another technique for capturing information to increase the understanding of current situations. This technique can be used for breaking down complex decisions and vaguely defined changing situations that have created the messiness found in the currently analyzed situation. Professor Jay Couger implies that decisions are made in increments and usually by trade-offs between different policy conditions in a situation.[19] Many decisions are based on policies; therefore, decision makers first need to determine the underlying policies regarding the decision. Then these policies are broken down into further refined increments for more effective analysis. At this point much more specific information is provided about how decisions were made that led to the situational messiness, and decision makers can then potentially identify the underlying causes of such messiness, at least from a policy perspective.

Many techniques use a combination of tools to further clarify the information about a situation. Most begin by asking a series of questions that lead to more expansive information gathering and analysis. The ladder of abstraction[20] begins with a brief statement of the current situation under investigation and then asks the following two questions: "How did the situation occur?" and "Why did the situation occur?" These questions and their answers create movement up or down in levels of abstraction. In addition, there can be lateral movement with the following added questions: "Why else?" or "How else?" Asking these questions of why and why else broadens the description of the situation, making it more abstract. Asking about how and how else presents the description of the situation in very specific, concrete terms. Schematically, the technique is illustrated in a general usage format

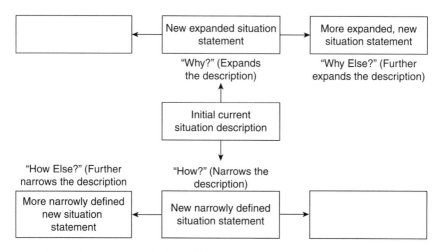

Figure 2.3 Usage Format of Ladder of Abstraction.

in figure 2.3. A more detailed example will be explained in the next chapter.

The why/why method, often called the "Five Whys," begins by asking a series of why questions: "Why is this situation happening?" "Why is there a problem?" "Why is this situation important?"[21] Taking the initial responses, a second series of why questions are asked about those responses and the rounds of asking why questions (usually no more than five rounds) regarding the preceding responses continue until decision makers are outside their scope of influence regarding the situation. In a tree-diagram format for general use, the technique would basically look as in figure 2.4.

Lots of information has been generated about the convergent list of messy current situations. The decision makers may now have experienced increased tension from acquiring and analyzing this additional information, and they may want to prioritize the initial convergent list differently or may be more strongly committed to the decision priority of the original convergent list. Assuming that new convergent thinking is needed, the decision makers can use several ways to prioritize the list including hits, highlighting, and hot spots.[22] Hits is an intuitive approach in which the decision makers review the situationally generated information and merely pick those situations that seem

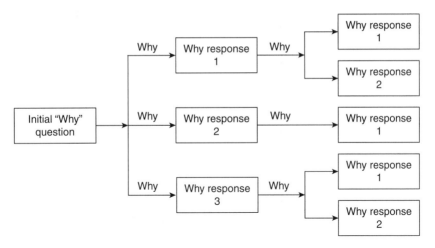

Figure 2.4 Usage Format of Why/Why Method.

most intriguing or interesting, or that just feel right.[23] Highlighting identifies the most relevant pieces of information in a situation first identified by hits, then clusters or groups the data into categories and names the categories. Finally, after using the highlighting tool, the hot spots or dominant theme of each cluster are identified and restated in relationship to the description of the situation. The final list of messy current situations (thinking element 7) is what the decision makers will use to mentally construct the improved, beneficial, future situations.

Decision makers often pursue the current state situational analysis through the convergent list (thinking element 4) and include only the final prioritized list (thinking element 7) before they begin to think about corresponding future state situations. The consequence and feedback analyses (elements 5 and 6) relating to the messy current state situation are often left out. If the "must" evaluation categories for the strategic goals and objectives and/or end-state key performance outcomes are causing extremely messy conditions, then these two types of analyses (consequence and feedback) may require immediate attention.

This means that decision makers must assess the positive and negative consequences of letting the current conditions continue. The decision rules of maximization of major positive benefits, minimization of major harmful costs, or some combination of the two must be decided on. Feedback looping effects analyses must be performed, and this requires that decision makers engage in single-loop, double-loop, or triple-loop feedback analyses.

The following examples are intended to illustrate how decision makers might react to a current state situation that needs immediate attention and how they then create an adjusted future state situation after using consequence and feedback looping analyses.

For example, if you come upon a house that is on fire, you will immediately consider the consequences of letting the fire continue to burn or of trying to put it out, and you will also try to seek additional feedback about whether someone is still in the house. Likewise, if you have an invention and have shown it to a few friends and they now want to order 15 of your invention, you are going to have to consider the consequences of trying to meet their requests and will seek additional feedback related to their requests, such as when they want delivery of the items. That is, crucial conditions in the current situation require you to consider all seven thinking framework elements and make creation of an adjusted future state situation paramount. In the two examples this means that you immediately call the fire department and/or rush to get people out of the house, or you start to build 15 pieces of your invention to get relief from the nagging of your friends.

Summary of Current State Situational Analysis

The primary question addressed in this type of analysis is whether the current situation presents enough conditions that trigger a need or desire to change it to a future situation. There are two key investigative issues necessary for answering that question. First, lots of information about both actual and perceived conditions in the current situation must be gathered.

Second, the analysis of these conditions must progress through the three-phase sequential information-gathering and analysis thinking protocols of identification, clarification, and prioritization. The identification protocol is to be used to gather preliminary information in order to understand which conditions are triggering the need for change. The clarification protocol provides an in-depth analysis of the identified triggering conditions. The prioritization protocol is an assessment for ranking the various triggering conditions as well as the situations themselves.

Decision makers can use most of the seven thinking elements framework in connection with various tools and techniques related to performing the three-phase thinking protocols to fully execute this step. Assuming that this analysis is handled properly and the final, prioritized list of current situations needing change is available as thinking element 7 in the framework, decision makers then must begin the anticipatory and visionary thinking and analysis of the corresponding, future state situations.

Introduction to Future State Situational Analysis

When you as a decision maker take on this form of future state situational analysis, you need to train your brain to think differently. Performing a current state situational analysis required thinking to be oriented in the present tense, that is, most of the thinking was directed at actual rather than perceived messy current situational conditions. Future state situational analysis presents a description of an imagined state future in which the current mess-producing situational conditions have been mainly resolved and the irritations surrounding those conditions have greatly diminished or vanished. Decision makers begin with identifying a general notion of what is desired in this future situation and then clarify it and develop a more specific vision of the new desired end results. This description portrays a place the decision makers want to get to, but it does not yet tell the decision makers how to get there; in other words, the description is not a solution. The purpose of this analysis is to identify, clarify, and prioritize the situational conditions the decision makers want to attain in the future and also to consider those conditions that could lead to the desired future situation not being attained. This is all indicative of a state of mind—of a mental, imaginary state the decision maker wants to attain.

Application of the seven thinking elements framework in this situational analysis begins with the first element of setting the outcome expectations for change by creating a dream, desire, or vision that is different from the current situation. Resetting or establishing different strategic goals and objectives and/or end-state key performance outcomes or even just creating new situational environmental conditions can be three ways to create the first thinking framework element. Applying the clarification thinking protocol, these newly established strategic goals and objectives or end-state key performance outcomes now creates a singular lens through which creative thinking efforts can be focused.

The divergent/evaluation criteria/convergent thinking dynamic is still here, and there is also a need to consider potential consequences associated with trying to achieve different strategic goals and objectives and/or end-state future performance outcomes. Consequence analysis and feedback looping analyses will also be a part of this future state situational analysis. The divergent, creative thinking element of this analysis (thinking element 2) allows for examination of alternative views of different future situations. After evaluation criteria (thinking element 3) have been developed and applied to the divergent list of potential future state situations, the convergent list of future situations (thinking element 4) is identified and clarified. This tentative closure can be validated by using the consequence and feedback looping analyses (thinking elements 5 and 6); these analyses may also lead to further refinement, reprioritization, and different final decisions (thinking element 7).

Two techniques for starting identification and clarification thinking protocols for a future state situational analysis are the construction of a proper individual vision and of future-oriented goals and end-state performance outcomes. Michael Hicks, an acclaimed author, suggests that the technique of visioning is a type of thinking people use to create a mental picture of a future situation focusing on goals and objectives— and on creating opportunities—as the steps needed to make that picture a reality.[24] The process starts with looking at a set of prepared pictures or the decisions makers' own drawings that tell something about the way decision makers want things to be. Then the choice of pictures must be narrowed down to a select few that provide the best pictorial description of how things ought to be. Next, decision makers must articulate the desired aspects in words and then expanded upon this description by adding more details. The goal is a practical-oriented description of what the vision means. This practical, verbal description of the vision can be further deepened by asking what the vision can provide (goal achievement and end-state performance outcome achievement) if it is attained and why it is desirable to achieve it (the kinds of consequences then possible). By specifying goals and end-state performance outcomes, decision makers will have some measurement mechanisms to know whether and when the vision has been achieved. Finally, there has to be a strong emphasis on identifying the significant gaps between the current and the future state situations and how to close those gaps.

To become practical, visions must be translated into goals, desires, or end-state performance outcomes. Initially, these goals or end-state performance outcomes may be too vague for specific action, and pursuing these broad goals and performance outcomes can result in false starts, inefficiency, frustration, or no action at all.[25] Consequently, goals and performance outcomes must be further clarified; that is, decision makers must make sure that any goal or end-state performance outcome that is included on the final prioritized decision list has legitimacy and is workable.

Future State Situational Analysis and Clarifying Protocol Tools and Techniques

Storyboarding is a divergent tool used to create a future story in six to eight panels showing the sequence of significant events connecting the current state situation and its corresponding future state situation.[26] The current state situation is portrayed in the first panel using pictures, numbers, words, or anything else reflecting the essence of the situation. The desired future state situation is portrayed in the last panel. The sequence of steps in their practical order is then portrayed in the remaining panels. Key issues, outcomes, obstacles, or insights conveyed in words should be included in each panel along with the visual presentation. In groups, each member's storyboard is shared, and then a composite storyboard could be selected.

Wishful thinking, as a divergent technique, loosens up decision makers' analytical thinking and allows a degree of fantasy in taking unique positions on issues. In his groundbreaking work, Andy VanGundy developed the following procedures for the use of wishful thinking:[27]

- Develop a statement regarding your current situation.
- Open up the situation to all possibilities—assume anything is possible.
- State the alternatives (future situations) in terms of wishes or fantasies using a variety of statement starters: "Wouldn't it be nice if…" (WIBNI), "Wouldn't it be awful if…" (WIBAI), "I wish I could be able to…"; "What would happen if we tried.…"; or "What really needs to be done is.…"[28]
- Convert each wishful statement to a more practical one by again using statement starters like: "How about our…"; "Assuming that we could get around our starting constraint, what might be the advantages…"; "It may be possible to meet our wish, but first we would have to…"; "Perhaps our wish is not as far-fetched as we first thought; what if we tried…"; "Although I really cannot do that, I can do this by…"; or "It seems impractical to do that, but I believe we can accomplish the same thing by.…"[29]

The wishful thinking technique raises decision makers' sensitivity to the assumptions made in order to answer some of the questions posed by the technique. Assumptions place boundaries on how decision makers might gather and analyze information, and therefore changing assumptions may open up new ways of looking at and defining future state situations.

The technique for helping construct a vision is called the boundary examination technique.[30] It is executed in the following manner:

- Write out an initial description of the current situation.
- Highlight key words or phrases and examine them for hidden assumptions.
- Analyze each assumption to determine its cause and effect (consequences) to see if they are really relevant.
- A new future state situation can be defined after the relevant assumptions of the current state situation are more deeply understood and replaced by other assumptions developed in response to questions such as: "What else might be going on here . . . ?"; "What would each stakeholder in a situation (current and future) see and what might be their assumptions or perspectives?"; "Where else might we find relevant information?"; "Are there common themes here?"; "What information have we not considered before?"; and "What data based on what assumptions provides the greatest insight into the situations?"[31]

The purpose of the goal orientation technique is to identify different goals or end-state performance outcomes tied to very specific aspects of situations.[32] The process of using this technique to define or redefine a future state situation goal or performance outcome helps identify what goals or performance outcomes must be achieved or tried to deal with future situational needs, obstacles, and constraints. These new goal or performance outcome statements must then be dealt with in order for the future state situation to materialize.

Hits, highlights, and hot spots were previously used as prioritization tools and techniques in current situational analysis. These same tools/techniques can now be used for prioritizing future state situational analysis.

Future State Situational Analysis and Seven Thinking Elements Framework

A number of tools and techniques were used to identify, clarify, and prioritize future strategic goals and end-state performance outcomes in future state situational analysis. After this first key thinking element has been dealt with, a divergent list of future situations has been created in the second thinking element. Then various types of evaluation criteria are developed for the third thinking element. These evaluation criteria are blended with critical thinking to produce a smaller but more reasonable and feasible list in thinking element 4. The list includes future state situations that still have a connection to the original messy current situation. This convergent list of potential future state situations is then subjected to further evaluation by means of consequence analysis in the fifth thinking element. After the consequence analysis has been developed for each convergent future state situation, a decision rule to either maximize the major positive consequences of that future state situation or minimize the major negative consequences, or perform some combination of both rules is chosen. The next-to-last thinking framework element involves performing feedback looping analysis on each future state situation on the convergent list. Based on the analysis of feedback looping effects, additional refinement, reprioritization, and/or different selection of future state situations may take place in the seventh element, and a final, prioritized, future state situation list is created. This is the list of future state situations that will be the focus of most of the thinking in the remaining steps of the decision-making process.

Transition Journey Situational Analysis

Performing a transition journey analysis is one of the three major forms of analysis presented in this chapter. It is not done even in a preliminary fashion until decision makers reach the third step in the decision-making process and is not finalized until the fifth step in the process. Furthermore, even if decision makers have proposed a solution that is at the center of the third step in the process, they still ought to ask preliminarily how that potential future solution might be carried out, and this is the central focus of a transition journey. However, this analysis is closely related to the current state situational analysis and the future state situational analysis, and it is introduced here for that reason.

A transition journey represents a path or avenue the decision makers imagine for closing the gap between the undesirable current situation and its corresponding desirable future situation. The transition journey does not serve as a solution; it is merely a vehicle or path on which an eventual solution may proceed. For example, the CEO of a firm faces a current state situation in which the company's operating costs would be greatly reduced if a material that has a slightly toxic reading could be used in the manufacturing process. The material used is not approved by the Occupational Safety and Health Administration (OSHA), but might be approved if used in a limited amount. The CEO is waiting for OSHA's decision, and in the meantime has to decide whether a number of workers should be laid off in the future in order to reduce costs. If OSHA does allow the limited use of the material, it would also allow the material's waste to be deposited in a nearby river.

One solution the CEO could decide on would be to use the material and not dump it into the river until OSHA makes its decision. If this would be the solution chosen, then alternative paths or transition journeys have to be considered for what to do with the used toxic materials. One transition journey this solution could take would be to store the material in barrels. Complications would arise as to what to do if OSHA eventually were to decide not to allow dumping of the material. The CEO would then have to hire a firm to get rid of the barrels of waste.

Another transition journey or route to take for eliminating the waste might be to contact the manufacturer of the material and see if the material could be diluted with other nontoxic materials. A third journey might be consideration of digging an open-air catch pond and lining it with plastic. The material could then be exposed to possible evaporation.

Each of these possible transition journeys for a solution comes with its own set of unique situational conditions that could strongly influence a solution choice and impose its own independent decision-making process. In other words, the decision to take a particular path or transition journey to execute a particular solution may present its own set of circumstances that have to be analyzed with the application of the seven thinking elements framework. After this analysis, a particular solution may be deemed inappropriate because it cannot be effectively utilized due to challenges associated with its transition journey.

Overall Summary of Situational Analysis

Three types of situational analyses were presented in this first step in the decision-making process. The analysis of the current state situation is performed first because there is an actual or perceived messiness in that situation (the situation is not meeting strategic goals or performance outcomes or presents danger or dissatisfaction to people in the situation, or is not meeting normal necessities of doing business). Various triggering conditions direct decision makers' attention to considering changing that messy current state situation. For example, any TV newscast focuses on actual triggering conditions that create the news in a particular story. Sometimes broadcasters talk about perceived triggering conditions, but this is usually not the case. It is important to note also, that most of the time these newscasters will not propose solutions to the stories they report; they only report on the situational conditions or circumstances.

In most current state situational analyses, the decision makers are most interested in thinking through the first four thinking framework elements of preloaded strategic goals or objectives and/or expected end-state key performance outcomes, the creative divergent list, necessary evaluation criteria, and the convergent list, before determining the final, prioritized list of current state situations needing change and their triggering conditions. Only in very specialized and critical current situations will consequence and feedback looping analyses be utilized before the final list is created.

Throughout all these analyses, the decision makers will employ the three-phase thinking protocol of first identification, then clarification, and lastly, prioritization in order to fully understand the situational issues. Various tools and techniques have been identified to help the decision makers follow these three thinking protocols.

After determining the current state situations needing change and their respective triggering conditions, the ultimate, real purpose of the decision-making process is pursued in performing the future state situational analysis. In this analysis, the decision makers will identify, clarify, and prioritize the triggering situational conditions that might help attain and/or prevent the attainment of the anticipated future state situation. This is where real visionary, anticipatory, provisional, and inspirational thinking is required of decision makers. The two possible future states are either an adjusted future state situation that reflects an incrementally improvement of the current situation or a brand new transitioned future state. With either future state situational analysis, decision makers are encouraged to execute all seven thinking framework elements and the three-phase thinking protocols.

The combination of the two situational analyses (current and future) will allow decision makers to gather and analyze enough information to provide a comprehensive understanding of where the decision makers have been and where the future lies. Knowing the past messy triggering conditions can help decision makers see what to do to keep them from appearing in the anticipated future state situations.

The very preliminary transition journey situational analysis may reveal a whole different set of messy conditions that could affect whether the messy current state situation can be changed into the anticipated future state situation. It is not necessary to perform this analysis in this first step of the decision-making process, but it will become much more relevant in later steps. Again, all seven thinking elements should be applied in this analysis.

The Chapter's Thinking Completion Box

The purpose of this book is to improve the thinking process decision makers use to make decisions. There will be major decisions associated with each step of the decision-making process and with each individual phase in each process step. Generally, each step will utilize a three-phase thinking protocol and use all or various parts of the seven thinking elements framework proposed in this book. This end-of-chapter think-ing completion box represents a summary of what decision makers might want to concentrate on in thinking through this particular step in the decision-making process. Critical questions are posed to see if decision makers have thoroughly thought through the relevant issues.

1. Have you, as decision maker, been able to make a dis-tinction between current situations that you feel need to be changed and those that do not? For those you want to change, do you see them in need of incremental change (adjusted future state) or radical change (transitioned future state)?

2. Have you been able to specifically identify the current sit-uational conditions (state of affairs, circumstances, events, etc.) that are motivating you to recommend changing the current situation?

3. What are your specific thoughts about what the changed future situation and its situational conditions would look like? (You have to set aside your analytical, highly rational decision making you used to evaluate your current situation and instead use highly visionary, anticipatory, and imaginary but useful thinking in order to prognosticate the improved future state situation.)

4. Have you employed detailed thinking to first identify these two situational states and their respective situational con-ditions, then added more clarity to your understanding of these aspects, and finally, have you prioritized these aspects (followed fairly rigorously the three-phase thinking protocol of identification, clarification, and prioritization)?

5. Has your application of thinking elements from the seven thinking elements framework improved your

decision-making analysis for both the current and future state situations and their respective conditions?

6. Can you look at yourself in the mirror and/or come before other decision makers and explain specifically what you did to reach your decisions for this step? What are your major decisions for this step?

CHAPTER 3

Challenge Framing and Causal Analysis

I n the preceding chapter, the director of the play was confronted with a number of unsatisfying current state situations he has to think about changing into a better future state situation. Various situational conditions have triggered his awareness of the need to make changes for the future. These situational conditions were fairly visible events and/or attitudinal or behavioral circumstances in the situation. For example, he faced an actor who was unsure of his lines and wanted the script reader close by during rehearsal. He also faced the situation with the producer who indicated the financial condition of already being $20,000 over budget before the first rehearsal.

Clearly, the director has to think about how these situations can be changed. Most likely he would want to know why the actor is ill-prepared in terms of not knowing his lines and how to prevent this situation from recurring in future rehearsals and, more important, during the performance of the play. He would also be thinking about these same two questions regarding the budget overrun. Thus, the director has taken current state situations and their conditions and is mentally proceeding to transform them into improved future state situations.

This transformation means decision makers mentally need to go beyond consideration of situational conditions. While the initial questions are how and why did these current situational conditions occur, these are not the most important questions to ask. If decision makers have applied the thinking protocol of identifying, clarifying, and prioritizing the future state situations and their situational conditions as part of the preceding step, the really important questions now should focus on what could prevent those future state situations from happening or what might be done to improve those future state situations and to understand their underlying causes.

Decision makers must be aware that the thinking focus has shifted away from current state situations to future state situations and away from considering situational conditions to now considering situational challenges. Answering the previously mentioned questions leads to performing the two major phased activities of this chapter—framing the situational challenges and then analyzing their causes. Situational challenges are underlying reasons, factors, events, and/or issues that could have caused the situational conditions or factors answering how those situational conditions came into being.

For example, an employee could take a look at the situational conditions surrounding her immediate job and could identify a number of challenges arising from the job condition. Maybe the job does not pay enough to support the lifestyle she wants. Maybe there is a lack of feedback and leadership from her immediate manager, an excessive workload that is disproportionate to the time given for completion, or a computer system that is antiquated and does not operate as it should. These challenges, in turn, can produce future challenges, and this is why decision makers needs to consider identifying, clarifying, and prioritizing challenges in both situational states.

Generally, challenges in either situational state could pose the risk of not allowing the new future state situation to be attained, or alternatively, they may enhance or improve the potential for that attainment. As previously stated, the director, upon seeing the actor not able to recite her lines, now has to think about why the actor does not know her lines and what it will take to get this actor ready for the next rehearsal and for opening night. This is both the director's and actor's challenge, and gaining an understanding of the underlying cause of this challenge may help attain the anticipated future state situation.

Just to be clear about what future state situation decision makers ought to be thinking about, let's review. If decision makers opt to make a complete change in the current situation, then the desired future state situation would have been labeled as a transitioned future state situation and most of the perceived and environmental conditions in that new future situation would be very different from the current state situation and its conditions.

Alternatively, at other times decision makers may want to make only minor modifications in a current state situation, which perhaps requires immediate attention. Modifications of these two types still represent something to be done in the future, and therefore they represent the adjusted future state situation. Making minor adjustment to current situations seems to be a dominant approach to problem solving and to decision-making practices. This is also why decision makers must be aware of and understand the major current state challenges and their causes. Only then can they prevent these challenges and their causes from also appearing in the adjusted future state situation.

In this chapter, the focus is on the challenges decision makers must address to realize a desired future outcome. These challenges could pose the risk of not allowing the new future state situation to be realized, or they may enhance or be required for the realization of the future state situation or even improve it.

The type of challenge that could possibly block or negatively affect the realization of the future state situation was alluded to in the previous chapter as a problem. The type of challenge that might potentially lead to positive outcomes being produced in the future state situation was labeled an opportunity.

In fact, there will be many pieces of information still connected to the original current state situation that will be transposed and then evaluated. Even though the focus in this step is primarily on challenges relating to a desired image of a new situation, some of the information from the current state situation will still be useful and necessary for informed speculation about the future challenges.

The three-phase thinking protocol of identification, clarification, and eventual prioritization of these problems and opportunities will require decision makers to engage in predictive, hypothesized, and visionary thinking. To comprehensively identify challenges means decision makers should have received enough accurate and informed speculative information about the challenge to be able to project what the challenge means, how and why it occurs, and who it impacts and how; finally, decision makers should be able to project various potential future consequences associated with the challenge under consideration.

After identification of the challenge comes definitional clarification of it. It is critical to arrive at a "true" rather than "symptomatic" definition of the challenge. Having a true definition of all expected challenges after they are prioritized then guides the second major phased activity of causal analysis that completes this step of the process. Having true definitions of challenges and their causes then guides decision makers in generating potential solution ideas in the next step of the process. These definitions are starting points for the serious decision making that will follow. However, if intensive creative thinking has been focused on generating a list of challenges and their causes, then it becomes necessary to prioritize this list because there will not be enough resources to handle this extensive list. All the decisions in the remaining steps of the process will ultimately be directed at dealing with these future state challenges. If the thinking and information about these future challenges are incorrect or deficient, then serious consequences, such as errors, mistakes, and even failure to reach the desired future state situation could occur.

Types of Challenge Categories

As mentioned in chapter 1, the simplest model of problem-solving and decision making included only three steps identified as: (1) identify and define the problem, (2) generate alternative solutions to the problems, and finally, (3) select the solution and implement it. The thinking enrichment and emphasis in this chapter is directed only at the first step, which is identifying and defining the problem, but "problems" are a particular type of challenges. The other major type of challenges are "opportunities". From a business-related perspective, challenges have traditionally represented problems and/or opportunities facing decision makers.[1] There may be other issues beyond problems and/or opportunities that decision makers need to consider as roadblocks or potential enhancers to attaining desired future state situations.

If the issue is a negative disturbance, obstacle, discrepancy, or deviation gap,[2] then there is a problem challenge. John Adair, a professor of leadership, defined problems as obstacles or difficulties in the path ahead of us and these obstacle-type problems can account for up to 80 percent of the problems decision makers may encounter.[3] The remaining 20 percent represent system-type problems in which there is a deviation from a norm. Professor Robert Mager and Peter Pipe, his business consultant coauthor, suggested that business decision makers usually find themselves dealing with performance deviations or discrepancies in personal interactions, clashes with policy, or unacceptable work practices.[4] These problems seem to cause someone grief, discomfort, loss of money, or imply an undesirable perspective about a situation. Decision makers should try to gather information by ferreting out the problem or discrepancy between what *is* (the actual current performance) and what *ought to be* (the expected or desired future performance) in an attempt to define the *true* rather than *symptomatic* discrepancy. It then becomes important to try to decipher causes of the discrepancy. If the issue has a positive beneficial potential and is not taking place now, but needs resolution in the future, consider it an "opportunity challenge."

Therefore, the first level of abstract thinking for defining a challenge is to distinguish problem challenges from opportunity challenges. This first-level distinction essentially categorizes a challenge facing decision makers as facing either anticipated negative deviations, discrepancies, or gaps versus facing the attainment of potentially beneficial anticipated opportunity-related outcomes.

There is a further level of abstraction thinking to consider for each of these two challenge categories. A decision maker faces "actual" challenges and then there are "perceived" challenges—that is, challenges not actually happening now but projected to happen in the future.

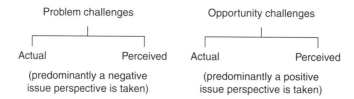

Figure 3.1 Level of Challenges Thinking Categories.

This actual versus perceived distinction applies to both problem challenges and opportunity challenges. These four categories of challenges are shown in figure 3.1.

In consideration of the four distinct categories of challenge thinking presented above and especially denoting the negative versus positive outlook to be taken when considering these categories, the following examples are presented. For example, sales were projected to rise by 8 percent, but sales this quarter actually came in at 5 percent, giving the sales manager an *actual problem challenge,* namely, a sales performance discrepancy of being 3 percent under the sales forecast. In another example, the budget still projected an 8 percent increase in sales, but the patent on the company's most profitable product just expired and two competitors have developed a similar product at a much lower price. The sales manager now faces a *perceived problem challenge* (the company will probably not meet the 8 percent sales mark because the competition and lost patent protection will likely reduce sales).

Consider the situation in which the company's R&D department has accomplished two things that could represent opportunity challenges. First, the department developed product X that has received FDA approval, no other competitive product is on the market, and a successful pilot manufacturing process has been completed. Now the company is ready to advertise the product, and the sales manager now faces the *actual opportunity challenge* of having to create an influential advertising campaign.

As a final example, consider the second thing the company's R&D department did. The department developed a new medicine that shows very positive results in offering a cure for disease Y, and no competitor has a similar product. Of course, further testing and approval is required, but the sales manager is now in a position of having to think about a *perceived opportunity challenge* regarding what to do with this new product.

There are some critical thinking-related assumptions made by decision makers when they attempt to deal with problem challenges. One common assumption is that managers should identify and address problem challenges that may keep them from attaining their end-state future state situation.[5] This implies that decision makers primarily concentrate on attaining some future goals, and therefore they should be proactive in thinking about what future-oriented problems could derail or negatively affect the realization of only those future goals. Consequently, only the future state situation takes center stage in the thinking about problem challenges and relatively little attention is paid to current state problems.[6]

There are other people who concentrate their attention on only current state situations under the assumption that decision makers should only deal with problem challenges on their doorstep because this is their current and only responsibility.[7] Thus, they focus their attention on improving a current state problem situation incrementally to handle the situation. This approach is reflective of the adjusted future state situation because even an incremental improvement requires thinking about what the anticipated improvement will have to be and what it is expected to produce in the long-term future.

In the end, prudent decision makers should probably assume that current problems, if left unsolved, will become problems in the future. Therefore, information about problem challenges having their origin in the current state situation but being resolved in some kind of future state situation should be analyzed.

Challenge Framing Formats: Questions versus Statements

Generating the identification and definition of challenges has been considered in one of two different approaches and either one of these approaches could be used to frame challenges. Management consultant

Tim Hurson recommends using "problem questions" that can be converted into "challenge questions" by merely replacing the word "problem" with the word "challenge." [8] His rationale for framing challenges in a question format rather than providing a simple statement of what the challenge represents is based on his thinking that questions represent a "call to action" to get an answer about what specific information to collect and analyze in order to more fully understand a challenge issue. His four original questions—What's the Itch? What's the Impact? What's the Information? Who's Involved?—were used to identify and clarify the situations that needed to be changed in the first step of the decision-making process. These four questions could be modified to help collect and analyze information about identifying and definitionally clarifying the future state challenges. The four questions would then be restated as follows: "What are the challenges potentially existing in future state situations that should be addressed?" (an identity question), "What might be the future impacts or consequences of these challenges?" (a clarification question), "What information about the challenge does the decision maker now know or should know?" (also a clarification question), and "Who is involved or related to the challenge?" (also a clarification question).

Likewise, William Altier raises questions that push decision makers to even more detailed and specific clarification about a specific challenge.[9] His questions are attempts to uncover significant, but hidden potential challenges that could go wrong, and they are as follows:

- What controllable and uncontrollable actions, conditions, events is this challenge dependent on?
- What other actions, conditions, or events are dependent on this challenge?
- In what ways is this challenge new or different from how it was done or the way it existed before?
- What in the challenge is based on inference, supposition, and speculation?
- What in the challenge is unchangeable, inflexible, locked in?

- Where does the challenge leave little or no latitude or margin of error for?

He also indicates that every ongoing challenge (problem or opportunity) found in a current situation has four fundamental characteristics that would be useful to assess to understand the challenges now existing in that current situation. Answers to these four questions could be extended to perceived future state situational challenges and could thus provide more definitional clarity about these types of challenges.

- An "actual" current challenge has an *identity*—it has information that describes *what is now happening*. By extension to a "perceived" future challenge, *identity* would provide projected information about *what could happen*.
- An "actual" current challenge has a *location*—it has information that defines *where* it is now happening. By extension to a "perceived" future challenge, *location* would provide projected information about *where that challenge could happen*.
- An "actual" current challenge has *timing*—it has information that defines *when* it is happening. By extension to a "perceived" future challenge, *timing* would provide projected information about *when that challenge could happen*.
- An "actual" current challenge has a *magnitude*—it has information that defines its current *extent*. By extension to a "perceived" future challenge, *magnitude* would provide projected information about what *that challenge's extent might be*.

Again, prudent decision makers would be asking both sets of questions about actual challenges in the current state situation and about the perceived challenges in the corresponding future state situation. It would probably be more important to understand the current and future state situational challenges if decision makers are going to have to deal with an adjusted future state situation. As previously explained, the adjusted future state situation essentially represents mentally a new and improved current situation where some of the current state situation's challenges (namely, problems) have risen to such discrepancies or deviations or gaps that now something has to be done to rectify those current state challenges. Thus, William Altier's questions about current state challenges and those addressing issues relating to his questions about perceived future state challenges can help strengthen the likelihood of the adjusted future state situation actually being changed.[10]

The other common format taken to identify and clarify challenges is to use "problem statements" that would be changed into "challenge statements." Professor Scott Isaksen and his colleagues[11] and Professor Couger[12] suggest using the following four-part format for preparing these statements.

- An invitational stem used to open up or invite responses generally begins with starter stems such as: How to...(H2...?), How might....(HM...?), or In what ways might...(IWWM. .?).
- An owner (Who?) that signifies someone being responsible for working on the challenge or following up on it.
- An action verb (Does?) that signifies a specific course of action envisioned by the challenge statement.
- An objective or object (What?) that identifies the target or desired outcome and direction for the challenge.

Examples of invitational stems for challenge statements are: "In what ways might the accounting department reduce its billing cycle to five days?" "How might the company get the newly developed drug Y to trials in a month?" "How can the project team better align interpersonal team relationships to reduce interpersonal conflict?" Closer inspection of these statements shows that they are questions rather than statements and that a little detective work has to be done in order to pinpoint what the challenge really is. These questions do, however, open up creative thinking rather than close it down, and they are slated toward identification rather than definitional clarity. Thus, it seems that both the challenge statement and challenge question formats use initial specific questions about actual and perceived challenges, and these initial specific questions can benefit the identification and/or definitional clarification of these types of challenges.

Challenge Framing: Application of Seven Thinking Elements Framework and the Three-Phase Thinking Protocol

The first of the three-phase thinking protocol for this process step has been the identification of the major challenges to be faced in the future state situation. This identification protocol begins with applying the first element in the seven thinking elements framework that specifies the absolute, predetermined strategic goals and/or end-state key performance outcomes. To naïve decision makers it may seem odd that the process of identifying a future state challenge starts with this first thinking framework element because strategic goals or performance outcomes should have already been set by senior management.

It is important to understand that one central objective of this decision-making process is to promote ethical decision making while also providing practical reasons for using this decision-making process. From a practical standpoint, all decision makers are usually asked to meet some kinds of performance standards, goals, or objectives. Senior management in the organization the decision maker works for usually has established a set of behavioral and performance standards and any issue related to the behavior of people working for that organization will be judged against those standards.

The first thinking element of preloaded strategic goals and end-state key performance outcomes has set the standards of behavior and performance expectations that are perceived to apply to a wide range of issues, are relatively inviolable and absolute, and guide behavior inside and outside the organization. Consequently, any time this first thinking framework element is used in any of the steps of the decision-making process, these preloaded goals and expected performance outcomes will guide the major decisions and remaining thinking elements of that process step. In practical terms, decision makers have entered this particular step of the process with a basic definitional understanding of its central issue (in this step, it is understanding what basic challenges are expected in the future state situations) and will be progressing toward developing a deeper understanding of this central issue as more of the thinking framework elements are applied.

In summary then, the components of the first thinking framework element would seem to be at odds with the three-phase thinking protocol of identification, definitional clarification, and eventual prioritization of challenges, but in reality this first thinking framework element acts as the standard and preliminary boundary against which all the other thinking framework elements and the process step's final decision output will be judged. Thus, regarding the completion of this process step, the question to be asked is whether the work of identifying, clarifying, and prioritizing the new future state situational challenges met the attitudinal, behavioral, and performance standards set by the major decision makers of the organization. In addition, some of the major goals and/or performance-related outcomes may also enter the evaluation criteria list (thinking element 3) as either inclusionary or reduction criteria.

The second thinking framework element consisting of using creative thinking to develop the divergent list of new future state situational challenges begins in earnest with the identification and definitional clarification of these challenges. The challenges decision makers need to concentrate on are actual and perceived problem and opportunity challenges. Decision makers need to identify those challenges in the adjusted future state situations or in the new transitioned future state situations that could have major detrimental or positive beneficial impacts on the potential successful outcome of those future state situations. In essence, challenges in those new future state situations could eventually cause performance shortcomings or performance enhancements in those situations. Performance standards or targets have been identified in the first thinking framework element, and this is the primary reason why the preloaded goals and performance outcomes of the first element must be stated first.

The most fundamental way to develop the divergent list of challenges is to ask basic questions about what decision makers actually observe (actual type) and/or perceive (perceived type) as causing performance shortcomings (problem challenges) and/or performance enhancements (opportunity challenges) in the future state situations resulting from the first step of the decision-making process. Actual and perceived challenges could also be identified and clarified by using the four characteristic questions suggested by management consultant William Altier and explained earlier in this chapter.[13] Essentially, these questions centered on the identity (describes what is or could happen regarding a challenge), location (defines where a challenge is or could be happening), timing (defines when a challenge is happening or when it could happen), and magnitude (defines the extent of a challenge or what the extent might be).

The technique of boundary examination is used to question various assumptions used in defining a challenge.[14] These assumptions can either be restructured, smashed (drop an assumption individually or in combination after each has been identified), or reversed in order to provide a more provocative definition of the challenge and to clarify challenge boundaries that are often indistinguishable. Thus, this is a technique to use on an already identified challenge in order to achieve more definitional clarity through more creative thinking.

To use the technique, say, for smashing purposes, decision makers describe the challenge as currently understood, then identify key definitional elements to reveal underlying assumptions. Then decision makers analyze each assumption for its causes and effects and finally restate the challenge based on a deeper understanding of its elements. For example, if the problem challenge is that university budgets are increasing but state funding is decreasing, the initial assumption might be that if universities attract more students, they get more tuition that will make up for the budget shortfall. However, this assumption is challenged because having more students means the university will incur more capital expenditures for additional dorms, classrooms, and instructors. These are the high-cost items needed, and without additional funding they could increase the deficit. Thus, the original assumption was incorrect and smashed and had to be replaced by another one of what could really happen if more students were attracted.

Progressive abstractions can expand challenge definitions to higher levels of abstraction and generalizability.[15] This technique starts with a basic description of a challenge and then moves up through progressively higher levels of abstraction until a more satisfactory challenge definition is achieved. Repeatedly asking the question, "What is the essential challenge?" will lead to definitional clarity of a challenge and reveal the limits of the decisions makers' skills, technological resources, and/or sphere of influence. This is a technique that takes the blinders off decision makers' thinking and requires them to investigate the "bigger picture" regarding a challenge. A simple diagram of this is provided in figure 3.2 where two levels of abstraction are illustrated given the initial challenge of getting people to use a new software program to generate their annual reports.

Laddering is a technique that allows decision makers to move up to higher levels of generality because an initial narrow or limited statement of the original challenge prevents any novel ideas or perspectives from being considered. Alternatively, the technique can be used to move down to more specific levels when the original challenge statement is so broad that decision makers' search for novel

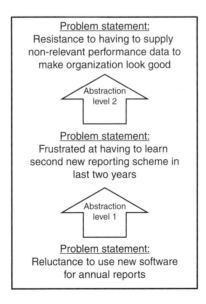

Figure 3.2   Illustration of Progressive Abstraction.

ideas flounders.[16] The ladder contains a top portion (the broader perspective) based on asking why (why is this challenge happening?), an initial middle portion (where decision makers are currently positioned regarding the original challenge statement), and a bottom portion (the more specific and concrete perspective) based on asking how (how is this challenge happening?). It is important to remember that the ladder has many rungs and can be extended laterally by asking the questions "Why else?" and "How else?" for any rung. Figure 3.3 presents this format with the example of one of the director's challenges.

In the example, the director faced the current situational condition of an actor tripping over a rug when entering the stage. The initial invitational stem for the challenge statement using the approach presented by Isaksen and colleagues could be as follows "How might the stage be redesigned so that actors entering and leaving it cannot trip over rug props?"[17] Through asking how actors can avoid tripping over rugs, the problem statement becomes more specific and concrete. One response might be to nail down the rugs, and the new problem statement then becomes: "Do we nail all four corners?" A problem statement based on asking how else the problem can be solved could be "Could painting a replica of a rug on the stage floor work just as well?"

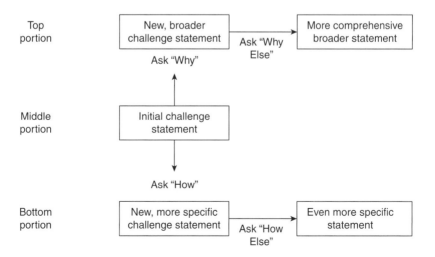

Figure 3.3 Laddering Technique Used for Challenges.

Asking "Why be concerned about the rug design for the stage?" might lead to the following response: "Tripping over a rug might injure an actor and keep the actor from performing in the play." This response could lead to a new problem challenge statement: "How many backup actors do we have for the play?" Asking about why else the issue matters might lead to this: "In what ways have we insured the play against potential personal injuries?"

Professor Tony Proctor applies the laddering approach in a slightly different manner. [18] He suggests that the top rung represents the strategic or highest conceptual level of the challenge, the middle rung represents the operational and managerial level, and the bottom rung represents the immediate and fix-it-quick level.

Either way of applying the laddering technique results in creative exploration of the identification and the definitional clarity of the challenges developed in the second framework element of the divergent list.

The next thinking framework element consists of the evaluation criteria used to reduce the previously created divergent list of future state challenges. As stated earlier in this chapter, various preloaded strategic goals/objectives and end-state key performance outcomes could be used to eliminate or retain challenge statements that reduce or improve the standards of behavior and performance expectations required for these goals and outcomes.

Other categories of either reduction or inclusionary evaluation criteria coming from personal characteristics and preferences and other environmental or organizational contextual criteria germane to the future state challenges need to be identified, clarified, and included in this third thinking element. Application of these evaluation criteria to the divergent list of challenges results in the fourth thinking framework element, the convergent list of challenges.

Challenge Framing: Creating the Convergent List of Challenges

The use of the 5 Rs approach (reanalysis, redevelopment, refinement, re-sorting, and reprioritization) begins essentially with the critical thinking used to develop the convergent list of future challenges. Hits, highlighting, and hot spots are three techniques already explained in the previous chapter as tools for creating the convergent list. Tim Hurson employs his C^5 technique to converge on his major catalytic questions after he identified and clarified his problem-related challenges with his initial four major questions (What's the Itch? What's the Impact? What's the Information? Who's Involved?).[19]

His C^5 technique begins with the cull element that is intended to separate out or delete questions on the divergent list that contain potential solutions rather than the identification and/or clarification of specific challenges in the question. For example, a question such as "How could policy A be used to solve the turnover problem?" presents a solution to our situation: we should use policy A. Consequently, this question is deleted from consideration at this time, but may reappear as a potential solution in a later process step.

The remaining questions are then clustered into similar groups containing around five related questions, none of which are duplicated. This element is used to avoid confusion and information overload and will force decision makers to expand their knowledge of their situations. Suppose the following questions are to be clustered: "What causes employees to not follow operational procedures?" "Why are employees complacent?" "Why is there a shortage of personal protective equipment for employees?" "Why were supervisors not watching employees perform at their machines?" "What is the percentage of supervisors having received safety training?" There would be two distinct clusters of questions here. The first cluster would constitute the first three questions, and the last two questions would form the second cluster.

The third element is the combining of these clustered questions into similar thematic questions. In the example above, the first two questions could be combined into asking the question "What level of complacency causes employees to not follow operational procedures?"

Following the combine element, the next element is to clarify, and it examines each cluster and names the theme it represents. Decision makers need to clarify the theme of each cluster by restating it in a way that captures the essence of the items in a cluster while still remaining a question rather than presenting a solution. Of the original five questions in the example, three questions composed one cluster and two questions composed another cluster. The theme for the first set could have been "operational issues" and the theme for the second cluster could have been "managerial issues." Clarification via a questioning format could have resulted in "What operational aspects of the work environment causes employees to not follow operational procedures?" The second clarifying theme could be captured by asking "What managerial aspects cause employees to not follow operational procedures?"

The final element in the C^5 technique is labeled choose. Decision makers here need to review all the prior work utilizing the C^5 technique and consider which questions or clusters look most promising, make the decision makers nervous, or are the ones the decision makers want to work on now. The decision makers may have to prioritize which questions or clusters will be worked on in order to complete this element in the C^5 technique.

Challenge Framing: Consequence and Feedback Looping Analyses

The next thinking framework element is to take each of the challenges on the convergent list and perform a consequence analysis (thinking element 5) on it using the basic question of "What are the expected consequences of the challenges defined and/or clarified in the initial convergent list of challenges?" This is, of course, an exercise in anticipatory, visionary, and creative thinking since the proposed challenges occur in new future state situations that have not happened yet. These consequences are the result of the thinking state of mind of the decision maker based on the analysis of information that has been collected and analyzed.

In order to get a more comprehensive estimation of a wider range of consequences beyond just evaluating positive and negative consequences, Professor Robert Harris recommends that decision makers think about long-term and short-term consequences, physical and social consequences, and direct and indirect consequences these challenges might create in these future state situations.[20] Obviously, the use of long-term/short-term consequences of a particular challenge depends on the time horizon imposed by decision makers. The underlying issue in using this consequence category is to get decision makers to think beyond coming up only with short-term, quick fixes for the challenges.

Physical consequences of challenges relate to the physical resources needed to provide clarity to definitions of the challenges, what the latter might cost, and what they might save. Social consequences of challenges are the consequences on the attitudes and behaviors of people affected by the challenges. For example, suppose employees are not following operational procedures. One of our challenges on the convergent list was: "Why was there a shortage of personal protective equipment for employees?" The physical consequence analysis would be asking how much this equipment costs, how many pieces are needed, and how much it would save in terms of insurance costs if all employees had this equipment. The social consequences would represent a measurement of the relief from pain, suffering, and anxiety employees would have if they had this equipment.

There are immediate and direct consequences felt by a variety of people (customers, suppliers, employees, managers, communities, government, regulatory agencies, etc.) if the challenges remain in force as they currently stand or come into future play. There are residual consequences from a challenge after a period of time and/or being transferred from one person to another or from one situation to another, and these constitute the indirect consequences. In examining a challenge-consequence analysis from an "if-then chain," the connection for a direct consequence analysis might simply look like "if challenge A occurs, then consequence B occurs." An indirect chain might be as follows: "if challenge A occurs, then consequence B occurs, which then has an indirect, but related effect of creating a consequence C." Again, using the previous example, the employees might receive a direct consequence of being in a safer work environment with the protective equipment, and indirectly the family of the employee may also feel better about their family member's safety at work.

The feedback looping effects analysis (thinking element 6) follows the consequence analysis after the consequence analysis has produced either a decision rule of maximizing and thus focusing on the major positive consequences expected from that particular challenge or minimizing the major negative consequences (the assumption is that the negative consequences outweigh the positive consequences and attention should be directed at minimizing the impact of the most onerous negative consequences) or a combination of maximizing the most important major positive consequences while minimizing the major negative consequences. It is important to remember that only the major positive and negative challenges come under scrutiny by decision makers when the decision rule is being determined.

Not only do consequence and feedback looping analyses help further prioritization and reduction of the number of challenges, but they continue the critical thinking and the 5 Rs approach started with the development of the convergent list. It is vital to define "true" challenges rather than "symptomatic" challenges because symptomatic challenges have the habit of appearing again shortly after all the time and resources have been originally committed to "solving" them.

Gaining some confidence that true challenges rather than symptomatic ones have been identified could be obtained through the use of a double loop feedback analysis. The use of double-loop feedback looping effects analysis would take decision makers back to considering the evaluation criteria, which is covered by the third element of the thinking framework. Decision makers want to feel confident that the values and assumptions used to select both inclusionary and reduction evaluation criteria could support these evaluation distinctions. Not being correct regarding these values and assumptions could end up labeling important criteria as inclusionary when they should be reduction criteria and vice versa. This may then cause further mislabeling of true as opposed to symptomatic challenges. In addition, if any of the values and assumptions of other thinking framework elements suggest a change in the actual outputs of these elements, then triple-loop feedback looping analysis has to be performed to correct the outputs of the respective elements so that true challenges will be the output of the challenge framing phase of this process step. True definitions of challenges are necessary for the causal analysis that follows and constitutes the second phase of this step.

Causal Analysis of Challenges: The Second Phase of this Process Step

In the first phase of challenge framing, decision makers have seen the extensive application of the three-phase thinking protocols of identification, definitional clarification, and prioritization as well as of all seven of the thinking framework elements. The final output of this challenge framing effort is a final list of true challenges in the newly adjusted or transitioned future state situations. The distinction between true and symptomatic is vital because the underlying true causes of these true challenges must be determined in the second phase of this step in the decision-making process. Identifying the causes of the challenges is not an exact science, and therefore there is not as much emphasis on using the seven thinking elements framework as there was in the challenge framing phase. However, there is an extensive list of techniques that can be used to identify root causes. These include Critical Incidents,[21] Pareto chart analysis,[22] K-T Problem Analysis or is-is not analysis,[23] chain of causation,[24] fishbone diagrams or cause-and-effect diagrams,[25] Apollo Root Cause Analysis,[26] and interrelationship digraphs or relations diagrams.[27]

Most of these techniques rely on the underlying 5 Whys (5 Ws) analysis of asking the question "Why are these challenges occurring?" five times in a row[28] or using why-why diagrams,[29] which were discussed in the previous process step. The 5Whys analysis is illustrated below and it starts with the initial challenge being identified; then brainstorming is used to find causes at levels below the challenge's starting points. About each subsequent cause identified decision makers ask why this is a cause for the original challenge. The answer is then used as a cause about which the basic causal question is asked again and so on. Professor Andersen's example of a situation where an opportunity challenge of having a low level of work in progress is occurring is illustrated below, and his causal conclusion is that the cause of having low work in progress is that the company has good relationships with its suppliers who are doing a good job of supplying what the company needs. [30]

> Original Situation: Low level of work in progress.
>> Why? Maintains no finished goods inventory.
>>> Why? Product has short manufacturing time.
>>>> Why? Plant only runs small batches.
>>>> Why? Plant gets frequent and swift supplier deliveries.
>>>>> Why? Plant has extremely good relationships with suppliers.

A relations diagram or interrelationship digraph could be either a qualitative relations diagram or a quantitative relations diagram. The uniqueness of a quantitative relations diagram is that a factor in the diagram could be designated either as a performance driver/cause or a results/effect indicator depending on whether more arrows point away from it or toward it. Decision makers in this case would identify a number of factors believed to be related to the challenge and place them into boxes or circles. Then causal relationships between the factors are identified, and these relations are illustrated with unidirectional arrows. The number of arrows coming into and going out of a factor are counted, and this then helps label the causal and effects factors. This is illustrated in figure 3.4, where factors 1 and 2 are considered causal factors because they have the largest number of arrows pointing outward. Factor 1 in this figure could be considered the root causal factor because it has the largest number of arrows pointing outward. Factors 3, 4, and 5 are considered effects factors because they have the largest number of arrows pointing toward them and very few, if any, pointing out.

A chain of causation generally looks for a single root cause and is simply diagrammed as shown in figure 3.5 as a sequence of cause-and-

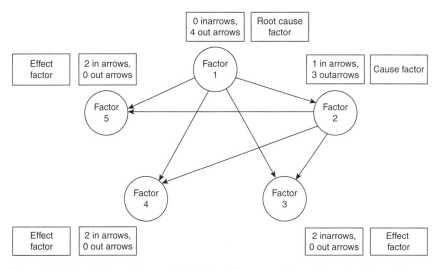

Figure 3.4 Basic Usage Format of a Relations Diagram or Interrelationship Digraph.

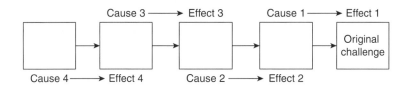

Figure 3.5 Basic Usage Format of Cause-Effect Chain.

effect events and suggests that a specific challenge is merely the end product of this chain.[31]

In constructing this chain, decision makers begin at the end of the chain (effect 1 = original challenge) and ask what the primary cause of this original challenge is. That cause (1) then becomes the effect (2) of the chain, and decision makers then ask what caused that effect. That is, they alternate the cause-and-effect relationships until they feel a reasonable root cause has been identified. Suppose that an announcement is made that the corporate office is going to be moved to a new city— why?—because there is a new CEO. Why does the new CEO want to move the headquarters? Because he lives in that city and has two young children and wants to be near them. The root cause of this challenge of moving the headquarters is the CEO's parental issue of wanting to be there raising his children.

Likewise, fishbone diagrams are useful to identify multiple causes of a phenomenon.[32] The challenge statement or concern is written at the head of the fish in the diagram and then usually four fins are created signifying possible major causes. Asking why anything occurs in these major causal fins produces more specific underlying causes, and ultimately decision makers have to determine which of these specific causes are root causes. For example, let's suppose that assembly line 1 is to produce eight model 2010 tractors on today's shift but has produced only seven tractors. What has caused the line to not meet its production quota? A fishbone diagram might look as shown in figure 3.6, and the root cause here was determined by the shift foreman to be the scheduler's absence, which led to many parts not getting to the plant on time.

Root cause analysis of very serious challenges usually takes considerable time and a team of experts to collect and analyze lots of information from suppliers, customers, workers, and anyone else associated with the challenge. The experts usually make recommendations to change conditions that have created the root causes of the

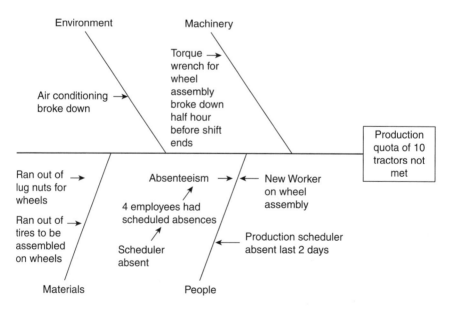

Figure 3.6 Fishbone Diagram of Production Shift Problem Challenge.

challenges they are investigating, and these recommendations are usually implemented.

Summary: The Challenge Framing and Causal Analysis Process Step

The chapter is intended to offer a more expanded and thorough approach to thinking and analysis for decision makers as they engage in the critical second process step of their decision-making responsibilities. In this step decision makers must clearly and correctly identify and clarify the challenges they will eventually have to make decisions about, decisions that involve committing money, time, human capital, and other resources to try to successfully deal with these future state challenges and attain the future state situation they envisioned. Decision makers identify and clarify the major challenges in order to find out what causes the desired or possible behavioral reactions to these challenges, what motivates that behavior, and what stimulates or might stimulate people to act differently. Identifying and articulating the underlying causes of a situation is a judgment call, but decision makers have several techniques available that can help them with this analysis.

Among other things, decision makers must carefully consider the future state situational challenges because they will make decisions regarding that future by changing current state situations into future ones that then will present their own sets of unique challenges. Decision makers must also distinguish between actual and perceived problem-related challenges and actual and perceived opportunity-related challenges in those future state situations.

In this step in the decision-making process, decision makers should apply the seven thinking elements framework thoroughly to framing clear and specific definitions of true challenges, to articulating consequences that extend beyond just positive and negative consequences, and to analyzing and carrying out feedback looping effects analyses and causal analysis so they can identify true challenges and their underlying causes.

The Chapter's Thinking Completion Box

This end-of-chapter thinking completion box raises questions about decision makers' handling of challenge framing (the first phase of this step) and causal analysis (the second phase of this step) of the future state situational challenges chosen.

Situational challenges are different from situational conditions, and decision makers must apply anticipatory, visionary thinking in order to identify, clarify, and prioritize challenges that could exist in the future state situations.

Challenge Framing Questions

1. Have you been able to make the distinction between situational conditions existing in the current state situation and its corresponding future state situation?
2. Are you able to distinguish between situational conditions and situational challenges in each situational state (current and future)?
3. Have you been able to divide situational challenges into problems and opportunities in both types of situational state (current and future)?
4. If your future state situation is an adjusted situation, have you recognized which current state challenges have a strong likelihood of also appearing in the corresponding anticipated future state situation?
5. Can you explain how current situational conditions might lead to future state situational challenges and how current situational conditions lead to current situational challenges?
6. Is the output of your analysis of challenge framing a list of legitimate actual and perceived challenges that are important in the current and the corresponding anticipated future state situations?

7. If you had to report your prioritized challenge findings to another group of decision makers, could you explain how you used the three-phase thinking protocol and, especially, all seven thinking framework elements to make your decision?

8. Do you have an understanding of why this challenge framing step phase is so important in the decision-making process?

9. Are you confident you have identified the true future state situational challenges?

Causal Analysis Questions

1. What investigative techniques have you used to identify the underlying cause or causes of your future state situational challenges?

2. Under what circumstances would it make sense to think about what causes are creating current state situational challenges?

3. Is it more important to push your analysis to identify a single root cause of a challenge or to identify a number of causes of a challenge?

4. If you feel comfortable that you have identified the major cause or causes of a future situational state challenge, how has this helped your decision-making and thinking-enrichment processes?

CHAPTER 4

Generating Solution Ideas

B efore getting to this third decision-making step, decision makers would have completed a thorough and accurate analysis of the previous two process steps. Completion of the first process step would have resulted in a list of current state situations and their conditions that triggered the desire for change to a more positive future state situation. This then required contemplation of the situational conditions that might exist in that future state situation.

The second process step led decision makers to identify and define the major current state challenges, usually assumed to be related to current problems or to current opportunities not yet attained; they were also to identify any anticipated future state challenges to understand their underlying causes. Particular emphasis is placed on making sure that major current state challenges and their causes do not appear in any of the two types of anticipated future state situations.

To illustrate the outputs of the two preceding process steps, let's suppose the manager of a fast food restaurant faced the following current state conditions: an absenteeism rate of 50 percent on Friday nights and 20-minute lateness for half of his staff on any given day. Clearly, these conditions need to be changed and improved if the restaurant wants to survive. The problem challenge the manager identifies is that most of his employees on Friday nights are teenagers and that most of his other regular day shift employees are single parents requiring babysitters.

The underlying causes of these problem challenges are that most of his Friday employees prefer to party rather than work Friday nights. Since they live at home, they are supported by their parents and need little income. The underlying cause of the 20-minute lateness problem challenge is that most of these single parents have more than one child to feed and dress before being taken to school or to a babysitter.

Obviously, the manager is thinking about utopian future situational conditions in which all assigned teenagers show up for work on Friday and no one was late for regular work. This would eliminate all challenges; however, a more realistic consideration of future state situational conditions might be to cut the teenage absenteeism rate in half and only have one or two employees show up 10 minutes late to work. Even these improved future situational conditions will bring future challenges and underlying causes that will have to be addressed.

As decision makers now start on this third step in the decision-making process, thinking now swirls around what is needed to solve the state challenges/causes in the future state situation and also what is needed to prevent major current challenges and their causes from recurring. The question facing decision makers is "What does it take to generate new, creative option ideas that can be converted into potential solutions that have real merit for realizing the anticipated future state situations?"

This thinking starts with decision makers creatively generating an extensive unfiltered and unlimited list of option ideas. These creative rough ideas will then be subjected to additional critical thinking in order to arrive at a fairly well developed, convergent list of option ideas. This list then becomes subject to different development techniques and the application of the 5 Rs approach of reanalysis, redevelopment, refinement, re-sortment, and reprioritization so a list of potential solutions can ultimately be developed.

The notion of having "option ideas" first and "potential solutions" second comes from the decision-making models developed by Couger and by Isaksen and his colleagues.[1] The first step of their two-step approach is to "generate alternative or option ideas"; these are choices that may ultimately lead to solution possibilities. The second step is to "develop solutions." Therefore, the three-phase thinking protocol in this step changes from identification, definitional clarification, and prioritization (used in the first two process steps) to generation, development, and eventual prioritization of first option ideas and then potential solutions.

Vital to the development dimension of the thinking protocol is how various types of evaluation criteria will be used to transform creative option ideas into potential solutions. Three types of creative criteria will be used to evaluate option ideas. Three types of business criteria and various personal criteria along with creative criteria will then be used as evaluation criteria to aid in the development of potential solutions. One of the essential requirements of this step is that some new and innovative option ideas must be generated and retained as potential solutions. Unless these types of option ideas are generated, there is little incentive to go beyond the initial obvious, rational, proven, and conventional option ideas. These old, conventional options were probably the ideas that ended up becoming the solutions that then created the messy current state situations in the first place. Applying old solutions to new challenges runs the risk that the same messy situations that appeared in the original current situation may then reappear in the new future state situation. If decision makers are dealing with new challenges, then it might be prudent to try new and innovative solutions. In the end, however, these new and innovative solutions must satisfy the criterion of usefulness as well as other criteria applied in the thinking elements framework.

Generating ideas begins with a highly intense group-oriented activity, normally brainstorming. Original ideas come mainly from people thinking creatively, not from machines or computers. More and better ideas can be produced in a group that has a large number of participants. Group leadership can set the tone for how ideas and participants are treated, how conflicts are handled, and how option or solution ideas are valued and rewarded.

Leadership in the group is invaluable. Many ideas initially are not fully formulated and ready to be used. Consequently, they are fragile and need to be nurtured and supported. This can be done when a leader encourages the group members to play with the ideas and explore different possibilities. The group leader needs to recognize that different thinking styles usually result in misunderstandings, frustrations, judgments, and conflicts between members. Yet, if the leader can get group members to listen to each other, to understand different viewpoints, and to respectfully question each other's values and assumptions, then harmony and civility can be restored in the group, and progress in creating novel and useful ideas becomes possible.

An additional leadership responsibility for a group generating ideas is to determine the group's membership. It is commonly assumed that having many members increases the chances of generating more ideas, that ensuring heterogeneity rather than homogeneity brings about a wider range of ideas, and that including people who are close to the issue will lead to more realistic and useful ideas. While these assumptions may hold true, group leaders may want to consider other aspects too.

Isaksen and colleagues suggest that the following four qualities should be considered as important for group members regarding their creative thinking capacity when generating any new ideas:[2]

1. Fluency: the ability to generate many ideas
2. Flexibility: the ability to generate many different categories of ideas
3. Originality: the ability to generate novel associations in order to form unusual or unique ideas
4. Elaboration: the ability to flesh out or expand ideas by adding more detail to make them richer, fuller, more complete, or more interesting

As a complement to the above-mentioned four qualities, Grivas and Puccio identify five styles of creative thinking that should be represented in a group formed to generate breakthrough ideas.[3]

1. Clarifiers are people who like to spend time analyzing and clarifying the situation.

2. Ideators are people who are big-picture thinkers and who generate big ideas.

3. Developers are people who focus on developing and perfecting an idea.

4. Implementers are people who are concerned with implementing the plan for carrying out the idea and then move on to the next project.

5. Integrators are individuals who have equal levels of creative thinking energy across all four styles.

It might be assumed that the only people needed in a group formed to generate and develop ideas would be ideators and developers.[4] However, this means not taking a holistic, forward-thinking approach that would make use of the diversity of minds, viewpoints, and skills previously mentioned. It should also be recognized that once this group is formed, it could be used in later steps, for example, when a group is needed to choose solutions or plan the implementation of the solutions chosen. This kind of group continuity may produce better results than forming different groups for different decision-making functions. Leaving out clarifiers, implementers, and integrators from the initial group formed for generating and developing ideas means that some of the decisions to be made in this process step may be put in serious jeopardy.

In order to pursue this step, decision makers first concentrate on generating option ideas that might be used to deal with the future state challenges and their causes in the situations they want changed. Since this is a creative endeavor, the generation of the creative thinking divergent list element (element 2) is the major thinking element that needs serious attention. Examining the preordained goals/objectives and/or end-state, key performance outcomes for thinking element 1 is deemed to be of some importance as it may establish some general broad boundaries for considering option ideas. However, decision makers, should be careful to not let these goals/objectives and/or performance outcomes bias the generation of option ideas. The techniques for generating these option ideas usually have an implicit or explicit prioritization scheme, thereby, leaving these option ideas with some degree of prioritization.

The divergent list of option ideas will then be analyzed using all seven thinking framework elements in order to develop and prioritize potential solutions. The element 1 preordained goals/objectives and/or end-state, key performance outcomes now become extremely important and many will serve as inclusionary evaluation criteria in element 3. The initial option ideas list now becomes the divergent list for developing potential solutions. The remaining thinking elements are needed to fully generate, develop, and prioritize potential solutions.

Generating the Divergent List of Initial Option Ideas

Creative thinking is needed to come up with new and innovative ideas that go beyond old, conventional ideas. Creative thinking initially generates the divergent list of option ideas. Generating lots of option ideas is critical because having more option ideas available makes for a better selection of eventual solutions.

The initial, unrestrictive divergent list of option ideas could contain old, conventional, mundane, rational, or impossible, innovative, unaffordable, novel, and tentative ideas as well as ideas for radical change or for incremental change. These initial ideas will still be rather raw; however, the purpose of the divergent list is to just get the ideas out for everyone to see and not to judge them yet. A number of tools/techniques can be employed to help generate the initial divergent list of option ideas.

Tools/Techniques for Generating the Divergent List of Option Ideas

Many tools and techniques have been developed to help people generate creative option ideas. The initial ideas are preliminary thoughts about how decision makers might respond to challenges in many and or unusual ways.[5] These unfiltered and unlimited ideas will have to be further screened, strengthened, sorted, and selected using prioritization methods contained in the techniques. The techniques for generating divergent option ideas mentioned by numerous authors[6] include attribute analysis, analogies/metaphors, brainstorming, brainwriting, checklists, morphological forced connections, problem reversal, 5 Ws/H, and the more mental-visual techniques of peaceful setting, role playing, and wishful thinking. Since any problem or opportunity challenge should lead to many option ideas, providing specific examples to illustrate each of the techniques and tools would become a monumental and lengthy task. Consequently, only the usage format of these techniques will be illustrated.

Attribute listing and morphological forced connections play off each other.[7] For the generation of option ideas decision makers would start with identifying the features of a current challenge or its causes, then define unique attributes of those features, and then create new, future state attribute ideas. These new ideas would constitute the creative option ideas that then could be developed into potential solutions. The usual manner for conducting this analysis would be to establish a listing matrix like the one in figure 4.1 for a new chair design. One option idea could be to change the padding from using foam padding to using jell padding.

Morphological forced connections can be used to generate a large number of option ideas for an opportunity or for an exploratory purpose. Using the previous chair example, a new chair design could be created in which the chair would have jell padding, an open spindle back, heavy colonial blocked legs, an aluminum frame, and a plastic covering. Remember, decision makers should generate new and innovative option ideas, and feasibility and workable solutions are not the main consideration at this point. There is a differing degree of creativity sought in the use of the two tools. Generally, attribute analysis focuses on one attribute at a time and subsequently, suggests a single,

Feature	Attribute	Ideas
Padding	#5 Foam pad	Bean husks, jell
External cover	Cow leather	Silk, sheepskin, plastic
Chair back	Straight solid back	Spindle open
Chair legs	Traditional spindle	Colonial block
Chair material	Wood frame	Aluminum, tubular steel

Figure 4.1 Chair Illustration of Attribute Listing Technique.

creative change in that attribute. This might be what is needed in making a change in an adjusted future state situation. Alternatively, morphological forced connections instigate a wider and much more drastic recommended change, much like the progressive abstraction technique might advocate. This technique might be more useful when trying to generate multiple option ideas to change to a transitioned future state situation.

The 5 Ws/H technique is an important questioning approach to aid individuals or groups in expanding their thinking about all related aspects of a challenge condition. It should be used in an iterative fashion by repeatedly asking the following questions: Who? What? Where? When? Why? In this way, a full set of options is explored exhaustively.

Problem reversal is another expansive technique for generating option ideas.[8] The first thing to do when using this technique is to write the problem or opportunity challenge in a question form (What can I do to reduce hand injuries in my plant?). Next, decision makers should identify the verb or action component of the statement (the verb would be "to reduce"). Now reverse the meaning of the verb or action component and restate the problem or opportunity challenge statement in question form (What can I do to increase hand injuries in my plant?). Now list ideas about ways to increase hand injuries (ideas left up to the reader). Finally, reverse the ideas on how to increase hand injuries, and now you should have ideas on how to reduce hand injuries in your plant.

Using metaphors and analogies can facilitate new perspectives on problems or opportunity challenges and can help decision makers getting mentally unstuck and come up with new option ideas. Metaphors connect two different universes of meaning where some degree of similarity exists or could exist between the initial item and its metaphor.[9] Use of this technique begins with stating the problem or opportunity challenge, then selecting a metaphor and subsequently using the metaphor to generate new option ideas. For example, let's take the case of a writer suffering writer's block (not being motivated and committed to sitting down and writing). The metaphor could be a world-class pit bull dog. The pit bull has the internal fortitude to never give up, being built low to the ground (short legs), having a robust chest with great lung capacity, and having a willingness to take on all comers. The decision maker needs to find out how these pit bull characteristics could revive the motivation and commitment of the writer to get back to producing written material.

An analogy is a statement about the similarity between two different things. Suppose a teacher wanted to improve her teaching. The analogy could be that a teacher is like a conductor of a symphony. By examining the characteristics of great conductors, she may generate some ideas that could improve her teaching. Michael Hicks uses the example of an organization and ant colonies by suggesting that both have life forms rushing about, both have a hierarchy of members, and both can inflict pain.[10] Analogies often begin with the question, "What is my problem/challenge/situation similar to?"

The final three techniques to be presented involve decision makers taking a mental and possibly a physical journey away from the situational condition they are currently dealing with so they can search for ways to let their imagination open up to creating new ideas. In the peaceful settings technique, people mentally remove themselves from the present surroundings in order to eliminate the constraints of their work environment that might be impeding their creative abilities. Often this requires moving physically to another location where distractions from work (phone, emails, etc.) are absent; people then close their eyes and get comfortable. They should then picture some peaceful setting and let the five senses (taste, touch, smell, sight, and hearing) allow the sixth sense of intuition to channel the creative process into ways to improve the condition they're dealing with. This is a practice of visualization.

Another technique used to bring a person's mind to imagine a different reality is the wishful thinking technique. Described by Andy Van Gundy, a renowned creative thinker, this technique assumes decision makers live in a fantasy world where anything can be done to deal with the problem conditions.[11] Decision makers then think of ways to make their contrived "fantastic" ideas more realistic; this is also a very useful technique for freeing decision makers from unnecessary and often unrecognized assumptions about the conditions they are dealing with.

Finally, role playing is another imagery technique. Decision makers here imagine being an expert with special knowledge about what to do, or they could imagine taking on the role of someone else in a different technical area having a different knowledge base (e.g., engineers could assume the role of salespeople).

Having generated a divergent list of option ideas decision makers must now develop potential solutions from them. Different types of inclusionary and reduction evaluation criteria become critical in turning the divergent listed option ideas into convergent listed potential solutions.

Evaluation Criteria Element for Potential Solutions

This is the first step in the decision-making process that deals directly with the concept of solutions even though these are still potential solutions. Creativity still takes center stage in their generation and development. All the major decisions in the remaining decision-making steps will be related to these potential solutions. If the appropriate solution is subsequently chosen and successfully implemented, then the future state situation this solution is to affect will not become the next situation needing change. The option ideas previously generated for its divergent list need to be carefully evaluated in order to be developed into potential solutions. Therefore, the evaluation criteria of thinking framework element 3 become critical, and it becomes imperative to apply several evaluation criteria sets to the option ideas presented.

One of the evaluation criteria sets to be considered is business related. The business-related criteria are reasonableness, feasibility, and practicality. The preloaded strategic goals/objectives and end-state key performance outcomes identified in the first thinking framework element and also the organizational-environmental contextual requirements mentioned in the previous two process steps constitute the set of business-related evaluation criteria. It is particularly important that these strategic goals/objectives and performance outcomes were reassessed in light of the anticipated future state situational conditions and challenges. It may be that these goals and performance outcome expectations were not changed drastically, but it also has to be recognized that past solutions were not successful in achieving those past business-related goals and performance expectations.

Recognition that past solutions have failed and that there is now the need to have new solutions is the rationale for the next set of evaluation criteria. Creativity-related criteria make up this set, and criteria included are: newness and usefulness.[12] Because the old solutions that were implemented earlier did not work in the current situation and the solution is being generated and developed for a new future state situation, the most relevant option ideas should emphasize some degree of newness as a minimum requirement for inclusion on the convergent list. This is not to say that every option idea has to be totally new; rather, even old and conventional ideas must contain some degree of creative newness. In the end, some evaluative judgment on whether an option idea can be turned into a useful potential solution has to be made. Usefulness and some degree of newness will be critical for the evaluation of creative option ideas.

Moreover, decision makers' personal evaluation criteria must also be included. Option ideas can be generated through individuals or groups interacting, but each person uses personal, self-interested, egotistical, and political criteria to advance his or her own ideas.[13] Therefore, the final evaluation criteria framework element includes three major categories of evaluation criteria to address inclusionary and reduction criteria.

Decision makers would most likely begin the evaluation of option ideas by applying the business-related criteria of reasonableness, feasibility, and practicality so as to satisfy the predetermined strategic and operational demands of management and the organizational and environmental requirements that are the critical factors to be considered in eliminating or retaining option ideas. The creative criteria are evaluated next, and each option idea is evaluated using critical creative criteria, such as newness and usefulness. The final set of evaluation criteria will be that of personal criteria. While the initial generation of option ideas is to be nonjudgmental, personal agendas of decision makers are involved in the final selection of a solution, and prudent decision makers should be aware of these agendas before making the final selection.

As a means of creating and retaining more creative option ideas, Grivas and Puccio propose the following questions in hopes that the answers still maintain creative newness and usefulness: "What can be substituted in these ideas to make something new?" "What ideas can be combined?" "What can the group modify about these ideas?" "How can the group simplify these ideas?" "How else could these ideas be used?"[14]

These are very similar to the following six checklist 5 Ws/H questions asked by Tony Proctor to spur creative thinking:[15]

1. Why is it necessary?
2. Where should it be done?
3. When should it be done?
4. Who should do it?
5. What should be done?
6. How should it be done?

Convergent List for Potential Solutions

A reduced number of option ideas are now on the convergent list after evaluation criteria have been applied to the divergent list, but these ideas still need to be expanded, developed, or fleshed out to become potential solutions.[16] This transformation requires tinkering, adjusting, polishing, reanalyzing, redeveloping, refining, re-sorting, and even reprioritization (use of the 5 Rs approach) in order to make the option ideas stronger, more targeted, and ultimately more useful. To pursue this further developmental process, a number of techniques are used to reanalyze and refine these ideas; they are then passed through a matrix in order to prioritize them.

The starting point for the serious conversion of option ideas into the development of potential solutions is to ask pertinent questions such as the following:[17]

- What are the strengths of this potential solution idea?
- What advantages come with this tentative solution idea?
- If this solution idea is implemented, what good things might happen?
- What spin-off ideas might result from implementing this solution idea?
- What issues will limit the effectiveness of this solution idea?
- Looking at the drawbacks and limitations, which ones present the biggest obstacles? How might they be dealt with and what might need to be changed in the solution idea so these drawbacks or limitations are addressed?

"How can things be made better?" seems to form the basis of many tools for developing and refining potential solution ideas. It is important to use these tools in an iterative process (repeating the process several times). This iterative process allows generative judgment[18] or affirmative judgment.[19] This is an assessment philosophy designed to improve the quality of examining the ideas rather than just either accepting or rejecting them. "How can things be made better?" is the essential question posed by this evaluation philosophy, and it is repeated and answered repeatedly. Tools utilizing this iterative philosophical approach include the following:

- ALUo: Advantages, Limitations, Unique Qualities, and Overcoming Limitations.[20] This is a technique that tries to keep new and innovative ideas in the mix. Identifying advantages or strong points of these innovative ideas is the first step, and in a group, these points could simply be written on Post-it notes and openly displayed. Next, the limitations, weak points, challenges, or areas for improvement must be identified. These concerns are generally framed as questions using starter stems, such as "How

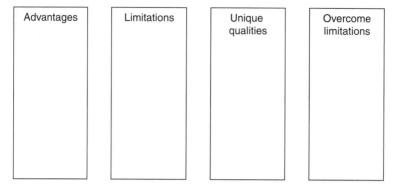

| Advantages | Limitations | Unique qualities | Overcome limitations |

Figure 4.2   Usage Format of the ALUo Technique.

to...," or "How might...?" The third guideline is identifying the unique qualities or novelty of the ideas by asking, "What does this idea have that no other has?" "What are some of the idea's unique qualities or aspects?" Finally, a return to the limitations developed in the second guideline is made by focusing energy and time on developing ways to overcome the limitations identified. Figure 4.2 shows an example.

- PPC° is an acronym for using itemized checklists (Pluses, Potentials, Concerns, and Overcoming Concerns) to evaluate one or more ideas.[21] This tool has both divergent and convergent thinking framework elements and is tailor-made for keeping novelty alive because *two rounds* of identifying pluses and potentials are completed *before* examination of concerns and overcoming concerns. As with the ALUo tool, group members produce information related to pluses and potentials, and then for the last two elements group dialogue ensues, and the more developed and refined potential solutions are produced as a result. Definitions of the tool's concepts are displayed in figure 4.3.

- POWER is an acronym for Positives, Objections, What Else, Enhancements, and Remedies.[22] *Positives* include responses to the following questions: "What's good about the idea?" "Why

Idea being evaluated:

Pluses (list what is good, positive about the idea—this is the final list after two divergent iterations).

Potentials (list what might happen if the idea was pursued, what are the possibilities; again this is the final list after two divergent iterations are performed before focusing on the next item).

Concerns (what are the weaknesses, shortcomings, or limitations of the idea—this is focused on only after the above two or more rounds of answering them is over and usually uses starter stems such as "How to…?" "How might…?" or "What might…?").

Overcome (generate ideas to overcome the concerns, starting with the most important concern and use divergent, creative thinking to pile up as many ideas as possible).

Figure 4.3   Usage Format for the PPC° Technique.

might it succeed?" *Objections* are responses to the following questions: "What are the idea's flaws?" "Why might it fail?" *What else* is concerned with the answer to "What else might be in the idea that has not been articulated yet?" *Enhancements* reassert the positives aspect via the question "How might the positive be made even stronger?" Finally, *remedies* respond to the objections aspect with the following question: "How might the objections be overcome?" The usage format for this tool is illustrated in figure 4.4; it consists of dividing a large sheet of paper horizontally into five equal columns for each of the five aspects. Alternatively, five separate sheets can be used. The title should be the selected idea, and all the information should be available to all group members so they can contribute their responses.

Highlighting and hits are normally used together and usually are considered as tools for selecting convergent lists.[23] Hits is a simple intuitive tool in which an array of ideas are listed and the decision makers then simply put some kind of identifying mark next to those ideas that are interesting and intriguing to them, ones that "feel" right, and ideally, ones that capture the essence of the situation to be dealt with. Highlighting combines this with a clustering approach. This tool

Brief Statement of Issue:				
P	O	W	E	R
Positives	Objections	What else?	Enhancement	Remedies
What are the benefits?	What are the flaws or weaknesses?	What more can be said?	How can benefits be enriched?	How can flaws be overcome?

Figure 4.4 Typical Format for the POWER Technique.

Criteria Solutions	Criterion 1	Criterion 2	Criterion 3	Criterion 4
Solution 1	+		−	+
Solution 2		+	+	+
Solution 3	+		−	−
Solution 4	−	+	+	−

Figure 4.5 Evaluation and Prioritization Matrix of Potential Solutions.

identifies the most relevant pieces of data (hits) and then organizes these points into clusters (clustering); the clusters are then named.

Finally, a tool called an evaluation matrix can be used to help *prioritize* the potential solutions on the convergent list. A reasonable approach to building this matrix as illustrated in figure 4.5 is to use the method advocated by Tim Hurson.[24] He simply puts the evaluation criteria across the top of the matrix and then lists the various solutions down the first column. He then evaluates each solution against each criterion using a plus sign if the solution meets the criterion, a minus sign if it does not, and leaving the cell blank if the person is unsure. It is important to evaluate all the solutions against a single criterion before moving on to evaluating all the solutions against the next criterion in order to minimize common evaluation distortions, such as the halo effect and contrast effect biases. A basic usage format of the evaluation matrix is presented in figure 4.5.

In the example in figure 4.5, the results of this very simple prioritization matrix would suggest that solution 2 might be a prime potential solution candidate and solutions 1 and 4 might be considered as backup solutions.

Consequence Analysis Element for Potential Solutions

In essence, two different forms of the convergent list have been blended. The initial convergent list consisted of a reduced number of creatively generated option ideas that resulted after the evaluation criteria were applied to the original divergent list of option ideas. These option ideas on the convergent list were then further developed into some initial, creative, potential solutions. This second list of potential solutions will be further developed and modified with the help of consequence analysis, feedback looping analysis, and tentative transition journey considerations.

Now that solutions, or at least potential solutions, are part of the decision-making process, decision makers should extend their investigation and thinking to various solution-related aspects that go beyond traditional decision-making models. They should exert their mental and theoretical energies to think in a highly provisional and anticipatory manner in order to create serious informed speculation about what these potential solutions might represent. This requires that decision makers commit time and resources to acquiring as much valid and reliable information as possible on which they can base their informed speculation about each potential solution.

Traditionally, a consequence analysis is not attempted until after a final solution has been chosen, a choice that would not be made until the next step in the decision-making process. Consequence analysis has been used in the previous steps of the decision-making process and will be used in this step as well. However, two additional, highly speculative consequence analyses will be added to the normal consequence analysis format in this process step.

Harvey and colleagues support the notion that any time a solution, even a potential solution, comes under serious consideration, two types of solution-related consequences need investigation.[25] One type of solution-related consequence is caused by the impact of a failed implementation plan on the organization. The other solution-related consequence considers the consequences resulting if a solution itself might fail. Both of these types of failure consequences could produce a large cash drain on the organization and/or a major psychological toll on the personnel and other stakeholders. Of course, if the decision making group originally included implementers, then the assessment of these two issues might not present as much of an issue.[26]

Making these consequence assessments now could provide enough informed speculation for decision makers to decide to drop a particular well-developed solution from further consideration because of the risks associated with its potential failure or with the failure of its potential implementation plan. Decision makers may make such a decision even before the amount of effort and costs for a solution and its implementation plan were not evaluated for these two failure consequences until much later in the decision-making process. This decision to jettison some potential solutions even before the last two process steps are specifically considered will mainly affect outlier solutions. The consequences about either anticipated failure of either the solution or its implementation plan must be added to the previous considerations of positive and negative, long-term and short-term, physical and social, and direct and indirect consequences. Then decision makers have a basis for better informed speculation before they arrive at the decision rule for each potential solution.

The consequence analysis decision rule becomes a very important consideration at this point. Obviously, decision makers want to advance only the most probable solutions that can successfully dealing with the challenges of the new future state situations. The consequence analysis has taken each proposed, developed, and prioritized solution on the convergent list and applied highly provisional and anticipatory thinking to evaluate a host of different future consequences.

Decision makers can essentially take each consequence and rate it as positive or negative in anticipation of the effect it will create. For the decision rule to be used, decision makers must arrive at an aggregate conclusion in order to determine the maximization rule, which suggests that there are probably more positive consequences than negative ones; decision makers then will improve or strengthen only the major positive consequences.

A minimization decision rule would suggest that a potential solution, in the aggregate, has been found to have more major negative consequences than major positive ones. Yet, a solution could become successful and be retained by decision makers if the major negative consequences could be converted into positive or neutral ones. The minimization decision rule serves as an example of decision makers applying the previously mentioned generative judgment[27] or affirmative judgment[28] assessment philosophy.

The final decision rule is a "combination rule," which means that it accentuates (strengthens) the most positive major consequences while also reducing or neutralizing the major negative ones. At the very least, decision makers will try to convert major negative consequences into positive ones. To decide that this rule is appropriate is a serious judgment call, and decision makers may need more feedback information before deciding whether to advance the potential solution. Clearly, a maximization decision rule is usually preferred over a minimization decision rule. There are two additional informational analyses that might impact the choice of the decision rule: a feedback looping analysis and the preliminary consideration of the transition journey of a potential solution.

Feedback Looping Effects Element for Potential Solutions

It is important that decision makers feels confident that the decision rule reached at the end of the consequence analysis thinking framework element is fairly reasonable, complete, and feasible. This decision rule becomes especially important in feedback looping effects analysis because it is the best representative of the anticipated results of a decision to advance or not advance a particular potential solution to the next process step. This positive or negative advancement decision can have serious consequences for dealing with the final two steps of the decision-making process. If the decision rule is positive, the potential solution is advanced and could become a serious contender for being selected as the primary solution in the next process step. If the rule is negative, the potential solution has little chance of being advanced.

More important, the consequence analysis decision rule represents decision makers' best appraisal of the results of a decision, and these results serve as the initial basis of evaluating any of the three looping effects analyses (single-loop, double-loop, or triple-loop analysis).

If a positive decision rule is reached, then decision makers have to choose based on assessing additional feedback information which of the three looping analyses to pursue. Each potential solution that has come through a positive consequence analysis should now be analyzed using double-loop and triple-loop feedback looping effects analyses. Double-loop feedback requires reconsideration of decision makers' underlying values and assumptions in making the decisions in each of this step's six framework elements. Triple-loop feedback would come back through those same framework elements and seriously consider whether the outcomes are logical and reasonable. The triple-loop feedback analysis may even require decision makers to go back through previous steps of the decision-making process and question their respective decisions, especially the future situational conditions and challenges/causes that the potential solution is intended to handle. Ultimately, decision makers will have executed single-loop (reconsidered all the prior ideas on the convergent list), double-loop (reevaluated most of the values and assumptions behind making the six framework element decisions), and triple-loop feedback analyses (reconsidered most of the previous framework element outcomes and even some of the outcomes of previous steps in the decision-making process). Finalizing the feedback looping analysis should help complete the application of the 5 Rs approach of reanalysis, redevelopment, refinement, re-sortment, and reprioritization of the potential solutions.

Transition Journey Preliminary Evaluation

Before finishing this step, decision makers should make a preliminary evaluation of the transition journey that might be taken with the remaining positive potential solutions. How to handle the gap between the current situation and its corresponding future situation leads to better informed speculation about what the transition journey of the potential solution might be. The transition journey represents a potential path of how a solution could be used to bridge the gap between the old, current situation and the new future situation. Decision makers need to ask "What is the most reasonable and useful path for this potential solution to take in order to reach its anticipated future state situation?" Essentially, decision makers are trying to evaluate whether there are legitimate means for the proposed solution to achieve its purpose. Speculating in an informed way about answers to the transition journey question will help decision makers think about the implementation plan that is required in the last step of the decision-making process. Assuming that the initial informed speculation results in a fairly positive evaluation of the potential solution, that solution becomes more credible and more likely to be added to the final framework element of strongest potential solutions to be advanced to the next process step.

Summary: Generating Solution Ideas

This is the step in the decision-making process that gets decision makers close to making the one decision the entire decision-making process focuses on: deciding which final solution will handle the journey to move from a messy current state situation to a new, improved, and positive future state situation. In order to make that final choice, a number of potential solutions must be available for selection, and generating, developing, and prioritizing a list of potential solutions off of an initial list of option ideas is the ultimate purpose of this process step.

The reasoning abilities of decision makers are stretched in this process step in a number of the thinking framework elements. Unrestricted opportunities to come up with any ideas were provided in generating the creative divergent list of option ideas. Developing the different categories of business-related, creativity-related, and personal-related evaluation criteria and segmenting them into inclusionary and reduction criteria was another thinking endeavor. Because there is no information available and no prior feedback information has been provided about consequences of the failure of either the solution or the implementation plan, the mental abilities of decision makers to arrive at these two consequence assessments must include visionary thinking. In addition, coming up with an aggregate assessment of the final decision rule at the conclusion of the consequence analysis really pushed decision makers' reasoning abilities. Finally, being required to consider all three feedback looping analyses in using feedback looping effects analysis created another great mental and reasoning demand for decision makers.

A very subtle, final requirement is to perform the transition journey evaluation for the potential solutions that could be on the final list of potential solutions. All of these extended thinking endeavors have been for the purpose of trying to provide decision makers with better informed speculation about which potential solutions have real merit and can become successful solutions.

Finally, it must be emphasized that the potential solutions being generated, developed, and prioritized to reach this process step's final list serve two purposes. One purpose for these potential solutions is that the potential solution chosen should be able to deal with the challenges and their causes in the new future state situations selected for change. The other purpose for these final potential solutions is that they must be able to satisfy the list of absolute, inviolable, preloaded, preexisting, and predetermined strategic goals/objectives and/or end-state key performance outcomes determined by management.

The Chapter's Thinking Completion Box

This is the chapter where creative thinking dominates. Consequently, decision makers have to become highly provisional, visionary, and anticipatory in creating informed speculation about what can be used to generate, develop, and prioritize potential solutions. These potential solutions create the matrix of solutions from which decision makers will next make a choice of the one solution to implement so as to attain the anticipated new future situations. If faulty or deficient input (in this case potential solutions that have not been well thought out) is entered, then the decision-making process will produce deficient output (in this case the solution chosen in the next process step will not work, and decision makers have to deal with another situation needing change). In terms of the necessary thinking for this step, be sure to:

1. Generate a large number of nonjudgmental option ideas first—any possible or impossible idea that might help achieve the new future situation and/or deal with the future challenges.
2. Seek contributions and opinions from a variety of people to generate option ideas.
3. Carefully but thoroughly apply all the evaluation criteria information from business-related, creative-related, and personal-related criteria sets in order to determine acceptable option ideas.
4. Again, use other people's contributions and opinions in order to convert option ideas into developed potential solutions.
5. Recognize that asking pertinent, tool-related questions enhances your thinking and causes you to have informed speculation of better quality about option and potential solution ideas.
6. Intense and extended future-oriented thinking is needed for failure-mode, solution-related consequence analysis, feedback looping analysis, and preliminary transition journey evaluation of potential solutions that initially have the highest possibility of acceptance. The risk of advancing faulty potential solutions is greatly reduced if information about these items is considered now!
7. Continuously seek to apply the 5 Rs (reanalysis, redevelopment, refinement, re-sortment, and reprioritization) and the generative judgment principle to potential solutions.

CHAPTER 5

Choosing a Solution Set

S uppose you are the owner of an auto recycling operation that buys junk cars and resells their used parts to a variety of customers. Your current state problem challenge relates to having a high return rate of these parts due to retail customers not really knowing specific information about their cars. That is, individuals or body shops are buying replacement parts, but their insurance companies require more information before they are willing to settle claims. If the replacement parts do not fit for the regular customer and/or insurance companies will not pay, parts are frequently returned, and the money paid back for returns reduces the profit for your company.

To change the situational conditions, you want fewer returns and more final sales. Your future state opportunity challenge is to get the employees at your sales counter and in your yard to be "synched" and identify and then obtain from the yard the correct part when it is first ordered. However, your sales counter people are paid on a commission basis for every part they sell even if it is the wrong part.

Among others, the following option ideas have been previously formulated:

- quit selling to customers with the highest return rates
- offer an incentive reward to the sales counter person ordering the correct part
- train every employee to inspect parts for damage

- decrease commissions when a part is returned or require a return fee
- hire an expert to verify if the part would work on a customer's vehicle
- require customers to provide the vehicle identification number (VIN) when ordering a part
- have a designated person check the part before it leaves or is shipped out
- have bilingual salespeople at the sales counter

After business, creative, and personal criteria were applied to the above-mentioned option ideas, the potential solutions developed from these option ideas were: decrease salespeople's commissions when a part is returned; train every employee to inspect parts for damage; require customers to provide the VIN when ordering; and finally, have a designated person check out the part before it leaves or is shipped out. All these decisional outputs were obtained in prior decision-making processes.

This step in the decision-making process includes three major activities for decision makers. The first major activity is developing solution success criteria. These criteria are the parameters in terms of standards, rules, tests, personal self-interest, resource constraints, or any other personal, organizational, or environmental factors a chosen solution must meet if the future state conditions and challenges and their causes are to be dealt with.[1]

After these solution success criteria are finalized, they then serve as the principal mechanism for evaluating the previous step's potential solutions and for selecting the final solution set that will contain a primary solution and one or two backup solutions. Both quantitative and qualitative techniques can be used in this second major activity to choose this final solution set.

The third major activity is to initiate the preliminary development of three control systems focusing on the chosen primary solution. The three systems needed are a monitoring system, a learning system, and a sustainability system. The primary initiation emphasis will be to identify the first two formal elements out of the four necessary to develop a fully operational control system. The remaining final two formal elements can only be completed after a solution has been put into actual operation.

As in previous steps, there is a recommended three-phase thinking protocol to be followed. The underlying purpose of the decision-making process has been to move toward selecting from a number of potential solution ideas the one best solution or solution set that will bring the new future state situation to a successful result. Therefore, this process step will follow the three-phase thinking protocol of development, prioritization, and selection and will utilize various tools and techniques to help achieve these separate aspects. It should also be noted that performing the three activities in this step will require using various combinations of the seven thinking elements framework.

First Major Activity: Develop Solution Success Criteria

Previously, solution success criteria were defined as the parameters decision makers want any final solution to comply with in order to meet the resource constraints, goals/objectives of the organization, and the context of the new future state situation that is to be attained. Developing these solution success criteria begins with applying the first four elements of the thinking framework. The preordained, strategic goals/objectives and end-state key performance outcomes utilized in the previous step will also serve as the first thinking framework element in this process step. The second thinking framework element leads to the generation of a lengthy divergent list of solution success criteria. A set of evaluation criteria, different from the solution success criteria, will serve as the third thinking framework element and will be used to retain or delete some of the solution success criteria on the divergent list. The retained solution success criteria, captured in the convergent list will become the final prioritized decision list (seventh framework element) for this first step's activity. In prioritizing the convergent list, a consequence analysis and a feedback analysis will be skipped.

Perhaps the easiest and quickest way to generate the divergent list of solution success criteria is to take a highly personalized, egoistic, self-interested approach. This self-interested approach lists for each potential solution from the previous process step everything decision makers want that particular potential solution to accomplish if it is to be deemed successful. Utilizing this approach even with a limited transfer of three to six potential solutions could result in an extensive list of highly diversified solution success criteria that would need to be prioritized to be manageable. Even this personalized, self-interested approach to generating the solution success criteria eventually has to revert to having some boundaries or targets that set parameters the solution success criteria must meet. The predetermined targets or goals/objectives of the organization identified in the first thinking elements serve as boundary and ultimately as a primary source of the inclusionary and reduction evaluation criteria for the solution success items listed in the divergent list that end up in the convergent list.

In order to demonstrate the application of the first four thinking framework elements to developing, prioritizing, and selecting solution success criteria, let's take one of the potential solutions recommended for the auto recycling operation mentioned at the beginning of the chapter. The auto recycling operation is facing a high rate of returned parts, and the potential solution we will use in our demonstration is that of requiring customers to provide the VIN for the vehicle they want parts for.

The decision makers are aware that senior management has preordained (element 1) that the return rate has to be reduced to 15 percent of sales and that any remedy could not cost more than $500. The decision makers think a divergent list of solution success criteria (element 2) could include emailing the company's commercial customers about this new requirement, posting signs or posters about the requirement at various entry points to the recycling yard, and making sure the company's computers have the software to show the VIN of all makes of vehicles. The decision makers might conclude that this potential solution could ultimately be successful if a directed communication campaign was established to inform all customers and employees about the new VIN requirement and the need to strictly enforce it. Two solution success criteria coming from the preordained element 1 information have to be evaluated in our example so far: first, the 15 percent of sales criterion and second, the $500 cost limit criterion.

Other solution success criteria could be developed for this potential solution and for the remaining three potential solution recommendations. The purpose of the solution eventually chosen is to reduce the parts return rate, and with four possible solutions with their own solution success criteria, the divergent list could be extensive and differentiated. This list now has to be subjected to the inclusionary and reduction evaluation criteria (element 3) analysis so that the number of solution success criteria is either retained or reduced.

The preordained requirements in the first element along with other organizational, environmental, contextual, and personal inclusionary and reduction evaluation criteria relevant to reducing the parts return rate are now used to evaluate the potential solution recommendation of having a communication campaign. Does it satisfy the 15 percent of sales parameter and the $500 cost limit parameter (element 1 issues)? If so and if other evaluation criteria are also satisfied, then the potential communication campaign solution becomes viable and the 15 percent of sales criterion and the $500 cost limit criterion are included in the convergent list (element 4) and they become relevant solution success criteria. This example illustrates how thinking element 1 issues can and often do become important solution success criteria too. Otherwise, if the use of the various evaluation criteria raises serious concerns about the communication campaign not being very effective in reducing the parts returns, then it should not be considered as a potential solution and the two previous solution success criteria might not be included in the convergent list of solution success criteria.

Some might argue that creating solution success criteria using the personalized, self-interested approach sets up a bias for the decision and therefore constrains creative thinking. Biasing complications, intended or unintended, could certainly occur, depending upon the approach taken. Creativity could also be biased based on where and when in the decision-making process the development of the solution success criteria begins. In this model of decision making, the full development of the solution success criteria occurs in the same process step in which the solution is chosen and this is consistent with other decision-making models.[2] Other models have developed solution success criteria in a process step prior to the one in which the solution is chosen.[3]

Creating solution success criteria in an earlier process step before the solution decision is made creates a biasing effect in the following manner. Since decision making employs a cognitive activity whereby cognitions are bits of information, establishing solution success criteria are themselves bits of information. As additional information becomes available in later steps, the previously determined solution success criteria may contradict the present conditions and possibly create cognitive dissonance in the decision makers. If the dissonance is strong, it is highly likely that the decision makers will focus on the initial cognitions and be biased against being creative and against accepting new information. Leaving the development of solution success criteria until the last possible moment before a solution decision choice is made attempts to minimize any biasing of solution success criteria.

However, a biasing effect can occur in the interaction between the first four thinking framework elements in this process step. Each decision-making process step begins with a target that represents the business-related, strategic goals/objectives and end-state key performance outcomes that are the focus of the decision makers' thinking and attention. These goals and outcome expectations are incorporated into vision statements; mission statements; strategic intentions; daily, weekly, or monthly performance reports; stockholder objectives' customer requirements' and regulatory requirements. They are supposed to have minimal influence on the creative thinking needed to develop the second element's divergent list of solution success criteria. Because the decision makers will ultimately be judged on how well the final solution meets these goals/outcomes, the decision makers will be biased to list the solution success criteria that can satisfy those outcome expectations.[4] This biasing effect was illustrated in the previous example.

The divergent list of solution success criteria now has to be reduced, and it is the purpose of the third framework element's evaluation criteria to help accomplish this. In addition to incorporating some of the major predetermined goals and outcomes from the first framework element, the evaluation criteria should contain criteria from other sources. A reasonable and feasible set of evaluation criteria requires input from internal sources such as decision makers' personal values, attitudes, norms, assumptions, experiences, judgments, and intuitions. There must also be input from external sources such as group social norms, organizational constraints, limitations, rules, procedures, goals and objectives. Input from environmental or contextual sources, such as decisions made by competitors, suppliers, communities, governments, and labor constituents, must also be considered.

Solution success criteria ought to be chosen because they seem to deal directly and successfully with the challenges previously identified and their causes. It is crucial that the final solution chosen is seen as reducing, eliminating, or neutralizing the causes of future state problem challenges; alternatively, it must be seen as enhancing, encouraging, or strengthening the causes of future state opportunity challenges. Thus, the final prioritized solution success criteria representing the seventh and final thinking framework element serve multiple purposes in solving challenge-related conditions in the new future state situation and help to achieve the expected outcomes related to various business and personal goals and objectives and performance expectations.

In summary, the selection and evaluative use of various inclusionary and reduction evaluation criteria identified in the thinking framework's third element and to be used to generate the convergent list of solution success criteria is critical. Obviously, a comprehensive analysis of all these sources could produce an extensive list of evaluation criteria.

In order to realistically deal with all this evaluation criteria (thinking element 3) information, a prioritization scheme must be established based on the following four factors: time, resources, intelligence and information, and consequences. All the major evaluation criteria generated previously could be collapsed based on these four categories and then used to determine the solution success criteria and ultimately, the potential solutions. A solution could be deemed successful if it meets a *timeline*, otherwise it would not be deemed successful. Likewise, if there are sufficient *resources*, the solution could be successful. If there is sufficient *intelligence and information* to meet or exceed the risks and if the *consequences* of the solution create more benefits than disadvantages, then the solution could be deemed successful. Decision makers have to rank these factors and then make decisions to accept or reject the solution success criteria if some of the questions about these factors are not answered in the affirmative. Notice also that asking and assessing these four factors constitute modified consequence and feedback analyses, which means no separate consequence analysis and feedback looping analysis are required.

Tools/Techniques for Developing Solution Success Criteria

The recommended procedure for the initial development of solution success criteria was to take each of the potential solutions from the previous step and in concert with the business-related, preordained strategic goals/objectives and end-state key performance outcomes begin to identify critical solution success criteria. This development process would begin with decision makers using "starter stem questions" such as the following: "Will it…?" (referring to the potential solution) or "Does it . . ?" These questions could include specific concerns such as: Will the potential solution work? Will it do the job? Does it improve present methods? Does it eliminate unnecessary work, increase productivity, improve quality, improve safety, improve use of personnel, improve working conditions, or improve morale? Is it timely? Is it a temporary or permanent solution? Is it too complicated? Is it legal? Are the materials available? Is it suitable and will others accept it (upper management, customers, the union, etc.)? Notice that these questions extend the boundaries beyond just retrieving factual information about what a solution might or might not do in achieving targeted business objectives and goals. Decision makers should ask these questions about any potential solution, and if a particular issue or concern associated with a particular question stands out as relevant and important, then that particular issue or concern could be further developed into a solution success criterion. Therefore, it is the above-mentioned questions and answers that help generate the solution success criteria.

The two techniques recommended next can be used to classify possible success criteria into major categories as a result of decision makers asking questions about a potential solution. CARTS is a technique used by Isaksen and his colleagues;[5] the acronym stands for *costs,* which are expenses associated with evaluating a potential solution; *acceptance,* which is the level of acceptability or resistance a potential solution may face; *resources,* a term referring to the kind, amount, and availability of necessary material, skills, supplies, or equipment for a potential solution to be implemented; *time,* which is the amount or availability of time for a potential solution to be executed; and *space,* which is the kind, amount, or availability of space needed in a given potential solution situation.

The authors of the *Harvard Business School Press Essentials* assess the value that any potential solution might contribute to important, business-related objectives/goals. They evaluate potential solutions using the following specific factors:[6]

- *Costs.* How much does the solution cost? Does it fall within the budget? Are there hidden costs?
- *Benefits.* What profits or other benefits will be realized? Will the solution increase the quality of our product? Will customer satisfaction increase?
- *Financial impact.* How will the monetary costs and benefits translate into bottom-line results as measured by net present value? Will implementation require us to borrow money?
- *Feasibility.* Can the solution be implemented realistically? If implemented, what resistance might be encountered inside and outside the organization? What obstacles must be overcome?
- *Resources.* How many people are needed to implement the solution? What other projects will suffer if people focus on this potential solution?
- *Risk.* How might competitors respond if this solution is chosen? What information is needed to reduce the uncertainty of choosing this solution? What would this information cost?

- *Time.* How long will it take to implement the solution? What is the probability of delays and the impact of delays on the overall schedule?
- *Intangible.* Will our reputation improve if the solution is implemented? Will our customers and suppliers be more satisfied and loyal?
- *Ethics.* Is the potential solution legal? Is it in the best interests of customers, employees, and the community? Would we feel comfortable if other people knew we were going to choose this potential solution?

As an example of applying CARTS to one of the potential solutions for the auto recycling operation, let's consider what categories of solution success criteria become important. Suppose the potential solution is to require customers to provide the VIN of the vehicle they are ordering for. The only real cost would be to obtain a computer upgrade (possibly also a resource) dealing with VINs if the company did not already have such a system (and not having such a system would be highly unlikely). Acceptance on the part of customers may become a serious issue, especially if customers did not know where to locate the VIN on the vehicle, and this may affect salespeople who have to listen to the complaints of customers who do not have the VIN when they attempt to place their order. Resources and space would be of low concern for this potential solution. Time may not be an issue for the company, but time in terms of a customer having to retrieve a VIN before ordering a replacement part may become a serious issue – the company may reduce return rates, but it may also lose customers. Consequently, acceptance and time-related criteria become important solution success criteria for this potential solution using the CARTS technique.

In general, the process of developing solution success criteria has received relatively little attention, but it can have dramatic consequences. The solution success criteria are the principal mechanisms by which a solution will be chosen for its supposed capability to successfully handle the new future state situational challenges and to achieve the targeted goals/objectives and performance end-state outcomes.

Second Major Activity: Selecting the Solution Set

This activity brings together the now available solution success criteria and the previously developed list of potential solutions. The purpose of this second major activity is to produce a final solution set that contains the primary final solution and at least one or two backup solutions.

To complete this activity, decision makers need to apply a quantitative tool or technique to choose the final solution set since the solution success criteria can now act as the inclusionary and reduction evaluation criteria and reduce the previously determined divergent list of potential solutions. Decision makers only need to create the convergent list of potential final solutions by running the analysis in a technical, quantitative fashion. This is what is often done; however, pursuing consequence analysis and feedback looping analysis along with incorporating nonquantitative confirmation techniques will result in refining and reprioritizing these solution set choices. Consequently, these two analyses and other techniques must be considered before choosing the final solution set as part of the seventh and final thinking framework element.

Many things as yet unresolved could derail the final choice of the primary solution. It must be remembered that the anticipated change the solution is expected to cause will occur sometime in the future. If this future is a long time away, then other issues of scarce or unpredictable resources, information, and consequences could undermine the primary solution choice and subsequently necessitate a contingent solution choice.

In addition, as Proctor suggests, decision makers should ask many questions and then analyze the answers for their impact before deciding whether to confirm the original solution choice.[7] These questions include the following: "Has there been serious, open discussion of the pros and cons of each potential solution?" "Have legitimate analyses been performed on the costs and benefits and strengths and weaknesses of each potential solution (a form of SWOT analysis)?" "Has financial and other quantitative information been used?" "Has the prior situation been reanalyzed in light of criteria and potential solution decisions?" "Has a potential solution selection been analyzed to see if new challenges might arise?" "Can the decision selected be justified and can solutions not selected be adequately and openly explained?"

After getting answers to these questions, decision makers must scrutinize each potential solution on the convergent list regarding its consequences. Given that the decision-making process will almost be completed after making the final solution choice and that decision makers' personal reputation for making prudent decisions is important, it is imperative to conduct a comprehensive consequence analysis for each potential solution, not just for the final solution. Decision makers must realize that these solutions should have been proposed to handle challenges and help achieve targeted, end-state goals and performance outcomes. This comprehensive consequence analysis will be a monumental task, and it must include identifying the positive and negative consequences, direct and indirect consequences, physical and social consequences, short-term and long-term consequences, and especially failure-mode consequences caused by the solution itself. Thinking about these consequences even though they may be tentative will be helpful in generating more informed information that can be filtered into this step's feedback looping analysis. Clearly, this feedback information and intelligence could cause decision makers to loop back to the convergent list of potential solutions and refine, reprioritize, and eventually redecide the final solution set.

Tools and Techniques for Selecting the Solution Set

At this point, decision makers have a list of solution success criteria that will be used to evaluate the potential solutions in order to determine the final solution set. For this evaluation process very simple or complex quantitative and/or qualitative (nonquantitative) tools or techniques can be used. It is important to realize that whether to use quantitative or qualitative tools depends on the information decision makers have: predominantly objective information about the context of the decision and the solution criteria or predominantly subjective information. Most business-related situations will include access to objective or probability-related information and would probably lend themselves to utilizing quantitative tools and techniques. If personal or business-related information deals with emotions, feelings, or other subjective information not supported by reliable and valid survey results or facts, then qualitative tools and techniques might be more appropriate.

There are numerous tools and techniques in these two categories of qualitative and quantitative methods for decision makers to use as they select and prioritize solution choices. A commonly used tool for selecting a final solution is an evaluation screen or matrix. The simplest matrices evolved from the technique of weighing pros and cons, a technique used for centuries under various names such as PMI (plus, minus,),[8] Evaluation Screen (pluses, minuses, blanks)[9] or Evaluation Matrix.[10] A matrix framework is usually set up in which the various potential solution ideas are listed vertically in the left most column and the solution success criteria are listed horizontally across the top of the matrix. The key to using the matrix is to evaluate all potential solutions against one criterion at a time before proceeding to evaluate the same potential solutions against the next criterion in order to prevent biasing due to the halo effect and the contrast effect.[11]

An example of a very simple evaluation matrix as illustrated in figure 5.1; in this example a homeowner is going to a hardware store to buy a wrench set. The Harbor Brand ends up being the wrench set to buy because it has been evaluated as matching three out of four solution success criteria.

Now suppose a numerical rating scale is added to a matrix to make it a little more mathematical. A woman is trying to decide where to get her hair and nails done. Salon A is determined to be the acceptable decision choice in figure 5.2.

A less quantifiable evaluation matrix could take the form of advantage-disadvantage tables[12] or utilize very simple standards such as meeting effectiveness standards (how well does the solution meet the goals/objectives you have outlined for the solution?); efficiency standards (which solution provides the most benefit for the least cost?); and/or simplicity standards (assuming the various solution possibilities

Criteria Potential set	Low price	Well made	Has all necessary sizes	Can fit both metric & std. nuts
Interlock brand		–	+	+
American brand	+		+	–
Harbor brand	+	+	+	

Figure 5.1 A Simple, Nonmathematical, Solution-based Evaluation Matrix.

Criteria Potential place	One person does both activities well	Reasonable price	Uses brand name products	1–1½ hours	Decision		
					Accept	Refine	Reject
Salon A	3	2	5	5	X		
Hairy safari	3	4	2	2			X
Sally's place	3	3	2	4		X	

Figure 5.2 A Simple, Mathematical, Solution-based Evaluation Matrix.

	Potential solutions			
	Solution method A		Solution method B	
Criteria-meeting standards of:	Advantage	Disadvantage	Advantage	Disadvantage
Effectiveness (achieved goals/objectives)		X	X	
Efficiency (benefits > costs)	X			X
Simplicity (Easier to deal with)		X	X	
Score	1	2	2	1

Figure 5.3 A Combined Standard Tables and Advantage-Disadvantage Solution Evaluation Matrix.

are fairly similar in their effectiveness and efficiency, which solution is simpler and thus presents less risk of unforeseen complications, opportunities, and failures). A simple matrix using the combined usage format is shown in figure 5.3.

Further mathematical extension of the basic evaluation matrix and inclusion of the distinctive categories of "musts" and "wants" criteria gets decision makers into decompositional matrices,[13] weighted systems,[14] prioritization matrix,[15] or Kepner-Tregoe decision analysis.[16] As an example of these techniques, suppose a young couple wants to buy a new house and start a family within a year and hopes to have two children eventually. They have looked at four different houses, and their agent would like to understand what is important to them and how each house fits their needs list. This example will closely fit the K-T decision analysis in which certain evaluation criteria are known as "musts." This means a house must meet this criterion or will be immediately eliminated from the selection if it does not. Criteria known as "wants" are factors the couple would like to have, and these criteria are weighted based on their importance. Ideally, the couple will hopefully be unbiased in rating each house on one criterion at a time. A score for each house is then calculated by multiplying the criterion weight with the rating of the house criterion. All the scores for each house are then totaled, and the house with the highest point total ought to be the one the couple is most interested in, as shown in figure 5.4. The Pearl Street house has a higher overall score than the Lory Lane house, and therefore the former should be the house they want to buy.

The tools and techniques and examples presented above represent generalizable approaches. There are more specific business-related tools for selecting, analyzing, and prioritizing potential solutions, for example, financial analysis, which stresses financial measures of value usually expressed as net present value.[17] In addition, there are payoff tables and trade-off tables for comparing the degree of variation between various potential solutions[18] and decision trees, which allow decision makers to see what effect a current solution decision will have on future outcomes.[19]

The final set of tools and techniques helps prioritize solution choices as the primary and/or the first or second contingent solution choices. Paired comparison analysis (PCA) could have also been used to evaluate and prioritize the solution success criteria.[20] This tool compares all potential solutions against each other, one pair at a time and usually

K-T decision analysis – house solution				
"Musts" evaluation criteria	Lory Lane House	Pearl Street House	4th Street House	Shady Tree House
Close to Grade School	Yes	Yes	No	Yes
Within 20 minutes to man's workplace	Yes	Yes	No	No
Has 3 bedrooms	Yes	Yes	Yes	Yes

"Wants" evaluation criteria	Weight (Scale 1–10)	Rating/score (Rating scale 1–10)	Rating/ score		
Freshly painted inside	6	10/60	5/30		
Sided	7	3/21	9/63		
3-car garage	5	10/50	1/5		
Exercise room	5	1/5	9/25		
Main floor laundry	10	10/100	10/100		
Less than 10 years old	7	7/49	9/63		
Modern kitchen appliances	9	5/45	8/72		
Total		330	358		

Figure 5.4 "Must-Wants" Solution Evaluation Matrix.

employs a weighting factor to determine the importance of one solution compared to another one. Application of the PCA tool to the previous housing example is illustrated in figure 5.5, and this time the Lory Lane house is the one chosen.

A less sophisticated prioritizing tool uses the sticky dots approach; this is most useful when decisions are made by groups of people. Each group member is given a specific number of votes in the form of sticky colored dots, and members then place their dots next to the solutions they value. Members are allowed to vote for just one solution by placing all their dots next to that solution. The solution receiving the most dots is the first choice, the one receiving the second highest number of dots is the second choice.

These quantitative techniques help select the final solution set, and if that decision is then buttressed by nonquantitative techniques, decision makers can be fairly confident that the best solution set has been

Solutions		B	C	D	Score
A= Lory Lane House	A	A2	A3	A3	A = 8
B = Pearl Street House		B	B3	B3	B = 6
C = 4th Street House			C	D1	C = 0
D = Shady Tree House				D	D = 1

Weighting scale 1 = Slightly more important
2 = Moderately more important
3 = Much more important

Figure 5.5 Paired Comparison Analysis Technique.

chosen. However, consideration of the issues in the next and final step of the decision-making process may still change the decision makers' primary solution choice.

Third Major Activity: Planning for Solution-Based Controls

Decision maker now have a solution set that contains a primary solution and some prioritized backup solutions. Further thinking about the solution decision needs to be moved on to planning considerations. Traditionally, the major decision makers would probably have left this process step after the solution decision has been made and delegated to other professional people the work on developing an implementation plan as part of the next and final step in the decision-making process. There can still be some things done in this process step by the major decision makers that could result in improved thinking related to the solutions chosen. These thinking improvements are related to the issue of planning as opposed to establishing plans.

For example, Tim Hurson offers a clear distinction between planning versus plans that seems relevant to the aim of this third major activity. He defines a plan as a thing, an organized set of data that is marshaled around time lines and targets, and he suggests that people unfortunately stick with original plans even when things change. In contrast, planning is about becoming prepared and understanding the material until its every nuance becomes familiar. He suggests that there are three values in doing proper planning: (1) it presents a way to learn what one needs to know to succeed; (2) it allows gaining people's commitment due to joint planning, and (3) it presents a powerful way to visualize success because the more planning one does, the more deeply ingrained that vision of the goal becomes, and the more likely people get motivated to make it happen.[21]

If thinking about solutions simply stopped after the solution decision was made, then all parties involved in the decision-making process would have no idea whether the solution had met its intended goals/objectives and/or performance expectations successfully or incurred failure or encountered mistakes. After all the work put into coming up with the final solution choice, decision makers should not be left in the dark about the outcome of their choice. Therefore, it seems reasonable to expect that additional thinking and consideration are given to planning various solution-based control systems by the major decision makers.

Normally, a fully functioning control system would contain the following four formal sequenced elements: (1) establish baseline goals/objectives/standards – the things the control system is trying to achieve; (2) assign some metrics to measure what is being controlled; (3) compare actual performance against the standards; and (4) take corrective action to meet the standards, if needed.[22] At this point in the decision-making process no solution is being implemented yet, thus, only the first two of the four formal elements can be dealt with at this time. However, it would be prudent for decision makers to begin planning what kinds of solution-related control systems could be set up at this juncture when a valid primary solution has been chosen.

Decision makers can reasonably be expected to devote preliminary planning efforts to setting up these two control elements (establishing baseline standards and then assigning metrics to each standard) for three different solution-related control systems. The first control system is a solution monitoring system; when fully functional, this system will generate feedback that tells decision makers whether the targeted strategic goals/objectives and end-state key performance outcomes the solution was intended to attain are met. Deeper inspection of this feedback information and continuing to monitor what is happening as the solution is executed could lead to improved understanding of specific errors, overlooked components, deviations, and/or any other factors causing problems. The first formal element of the monitoring control system should describe the methods, components, and tools needed to keep a solution controlled and operating at optimal performance. This is necessary because often solutions are executing actions for achieving new and changed conditions, and therefore they are essentially first-draft proposals, which makes anticipating contingencies difficult.

A second control system is a solution learning control system. This could be a totally separate reporting control system, or it could be included as part of the original solution monitoring system. Solutions are often not executed in the fashion they were proposed; thus, they may result in a failed attempt. Failure is a distinct possibility because of errors, confusion, or deviations among technical factors, process factors, timing factors, resource availability and usage factors, organizational cultural factors, and management-employee relationship factors.

For example, if solutions are to last a long period of time and require extensive resources and are also very new, it would be unrealistic to assume that they are foolproof and not subject to errors and needing corrections. The solution learning system would focus on learning about the mistakes associated with the solution not meeting its intended goals/objectives and performance outcome expectations. That is, decision makers would first have to think about what errors could occur and how to eliminate, reduce, or correct them; they would also have to consider how to improve circumstances so the mistakes do not recur. Second, they would have to assign metrics to these potential issues. With these first two steps, decision makers have some awareness of potential errors and what to do about them. This control system promotes learning-for-improvement as people deal with new and untried solutions.

A final control system, the solution sustainability control system, should be devised to begin assessing the sustainability of the solution once it is installed to make sure it remains in force and people do not revert back to old solutions and behaviors. This control system helps sustain momentum of change in the new future state situation. In order to design and implement a sustainability control system, four principal organizational resource-related elements have to be addressed. These resource elements, which become key components of the first formal control system element, include having sufficient and new resources as follows: (1) having additional training, data collection and feedback, consultation, and special meetings; (2) having a support system for people that provides them with emotional support and serves as a sounding board for their concerns; (3) having systems for learning the new technical skills and social skills and competencies; and (4) having new recognition, encouragement and praise programs to reward the new behaviors needed to sustain the change the solution was meant to accomplish. Lack of any of these resources could jeopardize the sustainability of the new solution.

Tools/Techniques for Planning Solution-Based Controls

Only the first two elements for any of the three control systems can be considered for design and development at this time in the decision-making process. Development of the first element (establishing baseline standards) is normally handled by asking questions about baseline items the decision makers want to monitor or want to have for sustaining a new solution. Although this seems to suggest movement toward a fixed plan, decision makers should keep the baseline items fluid and changeable, so that planning can continue while they are moving toward creating a fully established control system.

Decision makers then move on to developing the second formal element of a control system. This concerns measurement methods and calls for simple metrics. Metrics related to time, physical resources, people held responsible, percentage indicators, and coordination of different tasks could be assigned. Assignment of these metrics should not be taken lightly even if this planning is still only tentative because setting even preliminary metrics can bias thinking and possibly impede decision makers' motivational efforts later on.

The disciplines of quality management and project management have provided sophisticated tools that could be used to develop these control systems; among these tools are data collection matrices, control charts, failure modes and effects analysis, dashboard checklists, milestone analysis, Gantt charts, earned value management, fishbone diagrams, and Pareto charts.[23] Even though these sophisticated tools and techniques are available and could be applied by project managers or tech-savvy staff, for several reasons decision makers should stay involved and participate in developing the initial control system. First, the solution the three control systems are designed for is the one the decision makers have chosen. The solution's success affects their reputation as decision makers. Second, the decision makers are more familiar with the details of the solution, and if anything goes wrong with the solution, they are the ones who probably have the best insights into what to do.

The simplest format of a preliminary solution monitoring control system would be to include the relevant baseline standards (the first element of a formal control system) and their respective metrics (the second element) in a written report and include these elements in a single matrix or several smaller matrices. An example of a simple, usage matrix structure is shown in figure 5.6.

Solution monitoring system			Date: _____	
Solution name: _____			Prepared by: _____	
Solution owner: _____			Approved by: _____	
Baseline std item	Accountable	Key metrics	Frequency (when)	Corrective action

Figure 5.6 Matrix Structured Solution Monitoring System Format.

The first two elements of a solution learning control system could simply be attached as a written report to the monitoring control system shown in figure 5.6. Here again the central elements are lists of key people to contact, times to gather information, location or items to measure, or other indicators of performance or progress. Decision makers have to be creative to adapt the previously mentioned elements to the central issues of gathering feedback information for a monitoring control system, a learning system, or a sustainability system.

The preliminary sustainability control system would report on the planning for the four previously mentioned resources and their metrics needed to sustain a newly chosen solution.

Determine Final Transition Journey

Preliminary transition journeys were considered for each of the potential solutions finalized in the last process step. Now that a final solution set has been chosen, a much more concerted effort must be made to choose a transition journey for the primary solution. Detailed consideration of this transition journey will be carried out in conjunction with the implementation planning of that final solution in the next process step. This is why the transition journey development is still rather tentative in its formulation.

The transition journey is not the solution but the intended path or means for executing the solution. For example, if thousands of barrels of oil per day must be quickly transported to refineries, the solution could be to transport the oil by railroad. The transition journey component of this decision is then to determine which railroad company has the best offer in terms of railroad cars and well-maintained tracks to safely get the oil to the refineries.

The difference between a transition journey and the implementation plan is that the transition journey situational analysis sets the stage for the implementation planning; it sets the stage for the detailed thinking necessary to consider the different conditions and challenges that might occur on the path the chosen solution might take. As decision maker, before you can implement any action, you first need to know what the action will be applied to, what its purpose is. Determining what action to take is the transition journey. Determining how to take the action is the implementation plan. The transition journey and the implementation plan must be interconnected. Again using the oil transport example, decision makers have decided to transport vast amounts of oil to specific refineries in railroad cars (the solution) and have identified BNSF railroad as the company with the best and safest tracks and greatest number of cars and shortest routes to the refineries (the transition journey mechanism or means). Now the decision makers, in terms of implementing this solution decision using BNSF railroad as the vehicle for carrying out the proposed solution, must meet with BNSF officials to hammer out a contract, pricing, logistics, and many other details in order to implement the solution.

Deciding the final primary solution, then identifying and deciding on the final transition journey for carrying out the primary solution, and then addressing how the solution would be implemented using that path are three separate but interdependent forms of analyses. The first two types of analyses are completed in this process step, and the last one will be completed in the next and final step of the decision-making process.

Prudent decision makers are expected to have a final primary transition journey and one or two backup paths on which the final solution can be moved forward. Determining this final transition journey set also sets up a prelude to implementing the solution effectively because the decision makers will have already established a creative and well-researched agenda of possible transition journeys and can now focus on a specific implementation approach for a particular solution following a particular transition journey.

Summary of Three Major Activities for Choosing a Solution Set

The overall purpose of this process step was to decide which primary and backup solutions have the greatest chance of success in leading to the new future state situation decision makers want to achieve. Before the decision on the final solution set can be reached, decision makers first had to establish solution success criteria.

Given that a solution has now been determined in this process step and that this solution choice has personal, reputational, and motivational consequences for the decision makers, three control systems will have to be set up to provide feedback information related to the solution. Since only the first two out of four elements or components, of a formal control system can be dealt with at this point, the design of these control systems for solution-based monitoring, learning, and sustainability will be incomplete. Nevertheless, decision makers can begin thinking about what to include and establish baseline standards for relevant items. Second, they can establish measurement metrics that should be assigned to these respective standards to determine whether the solution is successful.

The three-phase thinking protocol implies development, prioritization, and finally selection. There is also variation in how the seven thinking elements framework is applied in the three major activities of this process step. Only the first four thinking framework elements are needed to develop the solution success criteria. There is a very close association between the first framework element of targeted preloaded, strategic goals/objectives and end-state key performance outcomes and the third framework element of inclusionary and reduction evaluation criteria.

The second major activity of choosing the solution set places less emphasis on the first three framework elements because the first thinking element of targeted preloaded, goals/objectives and performance outcomes also apply in this activity, the divergent list (thinking element 2) contains the previously determined solution ideas from the last step, and the evaluation criteria (thinking element 3) are the solution success criteria that have just been developed. The two analyses of consequence and feedback looping effects are the two framework elements receiving close attention in this activity.

Decision makers must deal with the inability to fully complete planning of the control system designs for the three proposed, solution-based control systems in the third major activity of this process step. Preliminary setup of baseline standards and measurement metrics is as far as decision makers can progress in this planning activity.

Now that a final solution set has been determined, decision makers must think more deeply about possible transition journeys the solution might take. Engaging in informed speculation about these possible journeys will be useful in thinking about the implementation planning of the solution in the next process step.

The Chapter's Thinking Completion Box

This is the process step that most decision makers think is the culmination of the decision-making process. They make the final decision by choosing a solution that they hope gets them to the desired future state situation. However, decision makers must stay involved and maintain their thinking engagement and the protocols necessary to successfully complete this next-to-last step in the decision-making process. Therefore, decision makers remained actively engaged as follows:

1. They must understand the important strategic goals/objectives and end-state key performance outcomes and how these items should influence solution success criteria.
2. They must not solely rely on using quantitative methods and techniques to make the final solution decision. Intuition, experience, and other qualitative methods and techniques become important contributors to this decision.
3. They must understand that even though this process step is probably the most quantitative step, asking questions to acquire more informed speculation about the issues and activities in this step is more important than the quantitative techniques.
4. They must understand and actively engage in setting control system standards and metrics for solution-based monitoring, learning, and sustainability systems even though details of these control systems can be delegated to other people.

CHAPTER 6

Implementation and Aftermath Planning

W ith the output of the previous process step, decision makers arrive at this final step in the decision-making process having made a commitment to a particular solution, developed preliminary yet deliberate thoughts about a particular transition journey, formulated the first two formal elements of solution-based monitoring and learning control systems, and identified four provisional resource requirements needed to sustain the solution. Once decision makers have made this final commitment to the primary solution in the solution set, then they must begin planning for its implementation and for control of that particular plan.

The implementation plan is an organized set of data focused on targets, resources, and timelines that spell out what is supposed to happen when decision makers put the solution into action.[1] The four sequential stages of developing this implementation plan are identified as follows:

Stage 1: Generate action steps

Stage 2: Aggregate resources

Stage 3: Align resources

Stage 4: Determine plan outcomes

Creating the implementation plan requires a continuous planning process in each of the four stages, and the planning process must continue even after the initial implementation plan is prepared because no plan is perfect or can take all eventualities into account. The planning taking place in this process step is known as "pre-implementation" planning. Ideally, decision makers will stay involved and follow through with fully developing monitoring and learning control systems for "during-implementation" and "post-implementation" planning. The entire cycle of implementation planning would include all three phases of planning in order to ensure that implementation of the primary solution is successful. Therefore, an ongoing planning process is necessary in preparing the implementation plan, and when appropriate feedback control systems have been developed and are providing negative feedback about the implementation, the original implementation plan may have to be revised.

This revision may come in one of two forms affecting the implementation plan. If the original implementation plan becomes subject to minor modifications or adjustments, then decision makers will have to recalibrate the original implementation plan. If the feedback information reveals that many major negative consequences are occurring in the implementation of the original solution, then decision makers may have to create a different implementation plan for one of the backup solutions. This second planning approach would constitute a renewal.

In addition to their tremendous thinking and planning investment in developing the implementation plan, decision makers must make sure that the implementation of the solution is progressing as planned. To track this progress, they must establish an implementation monitoring control system and an implementation learning control system to compare actual progress with the planned implementation protocol. This means that all four formal steps to establish a complete control system must be planned, and decision makers must gather and analyze continuous feedback information from "during-implementation" and "post-implementation" execution. Thus, decision makers have to stay involved with collecting and analyzing implementation feedback and they must have designed and installed implementation plan monitoring and learning control systems that are fully functional.

The seven thinking elements framework is used in this final step; however, its application will reflect some different and streamlined approaches. This is the last step in the decision making process and the one most neglected for a variety of reasons. Most of the previous steps have utilized visionary, diagnostic, and strategic thinking, but in this last step the emphasis is on tactical, contextual, evaluative, and monitoring thinking.[2] Many members of executive management may feel that their responsibility is to scope out the situation using their environmental scanning resources, to define challenges and future options using their extensive and abundant information channels, to evaluate and decide on solutions using their control and power over resources and then they participate reluctantly, if at all, in the operational and monitoring aspects of implementation planning. Their reluctance or nonparticipation in this last critical step may be based on the rationale that they can delegate this critical responsibility to project management employees. However, continued investment in monitoring implementation outcomes is still a vital responsibility of the people who contributed to the previous decision-making steps.

Moreover, two things streamline and improve thinking in this process final step. The first streamlining improvement has to do with a reduction in the number of steps used to create the implementation plan. Rather than the four succinct stages for creating the implementation plan of this book's model, many models contain six or more separate steps.[3]

The second improvement relates to acceptance planning. Acceptance planning identifies people who support the solution and those who resist it. A number of authors treat this planning process as separate from implementation planning.[4] People are pursuing change when they are dealing with the implementation of solutions. People have emotions and attitudes that direct their behaviors, and the proposed changes required by the new solutions could be frightening to them. Thus, for the implementation of a solution to be successful, one of the factors that has to be taken into account is this human psychological condition.

New solutions representing change and must be acceptable to many stakeholders to ensure the necessary motivation, commitment, involvement, and compliance for implementation of the solution. Otherwise, these stakeholders could demonstrate covert and overt resistance to efforts at implementing the solution. Therefore, acceptance planning leads decision makers to consider new solutions from the perspective of the solution's users, implementers, recipients, and bystanders who might be affected by the solution. Decision makers should prepare these participants and their context so they can accept the changes implied by the solution. Obviously, there will always be some degree of resistance against these new solutions and the changes they bring; planning for overcoming this resistance is an integral part of acceptance planning. Acceptance planning will become an integral part of stage 2 listed above, aggregating resources, rather than a separate planning process.

The three-phase thinking protocol in this final process step suggests a general format of planning, evaluating, and controlling, and this represents a change in protocol from the one in the previous step of development, prioritization, and selection. The thinking in this final process step has to be very specific and detailed in all four stages of planning. Each of these stages will now be described in detail, and the application of the various important thinking framework elements will be indicated.

Implementation Plan: Stage 1—Generating Action Steps

In order to transform a solution idea into reality, various action steps, including the tasks of carrying out the solution, are necessary. At this stage in the process, decision makers and a team of people have come up with a new and useful solution for their future situational crisis or opportunity. While some action steps may need to be done routinely for this new solution, many essential action steps will have to be developed as new components in order for the solution to be implemented successfully. The solution must be new to some extent because its purpose is to help attain a new future state situation that represents a change from a messy current state situation.

Various software packages can aid in recording and monitoring the progress of an implementation plan, but the original list of action steps necessary to implement a new solution must come from the thinking of people who are held responsible for achieving the solution outcomes. This mental listing of action requirements starts with the divergent, creative thinking process that has previously been employed in all the earlier steps of the decision-making process. These action steps are germane to what needs to be done in the solution, and they also have some satisfying performance-related impact on the first thinking framework element consisting of targeted goals/objectives and performance outcomes preordained by management or other decision makers.

Action steps are concrete and measureable activities that lead to a desired outcome.[5] Brainstorming for to-do lists can start with stem questions such as the following: "What do I/we need to do to implement...?" "What else do I/we need to do to implement...?" [6] How-How diagrams help people dig deep to identify specific action steps by first identifying general action steps and then repeatedly asking, "How am I /are we going to accomplish this?"[7] Schematically, this technique would look as shown in figure 6.1.

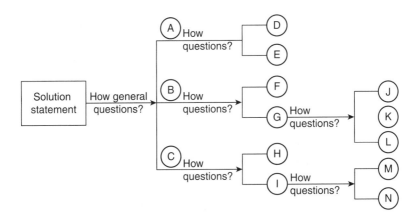

Figure 6.1   How-How Diagram to Create Action Steps.

As with other divergent lists, no judgments are to be imposed on the items making up the list. Evaluation criteria will then be used to help convert the lengthy divergent list into more realistic and feasible list of useful action steps. Many of the evaluation criteria will consist of resource and time limitations imposed by the organization, stakeholders, and the solution-relevant environment. For example, the implementation costs may be limited to $500,000, the project may have to be completed in one year, or another company may have to do the foundation work on the project because the original company does not have the necessary expertise. Additional tools for creating the shorter convergent list of action steps include Hits or the Modified C^5 technique.[8] This latter technique includes the steps of culling, clustering, combining, clarifying, and choosing. The modified version begins with clustering the ideas for action steps that seem to be related. Closer inspection of the various clusters may allow some of the steps to be combined into a more comprehensive step. These larger clusters now need to be named, and the individual action steps may need to be rewritten for greater clarity. Finally, and because of various requirements, certain clusters will be chosen and others discarded.

At the same time as this thinking about specific action steps for implementation is taking place, thinking about the physical resources needed for the specific action steps must begin. This discussion begins the next stage, which is addressed below.

Implementation Plan: Stage 2—Aggregate Resources

The resources for the implementation plan consist of a combination of physical and human resources. Physical resources would typically include energy sources; funds; time; materials; equipment; weather or environmental conditions; predetermined system, policy, or procedure boundaries or constraints; and decisions. Human resources typically include personnel needed to carry out the implementation action steps. Since the implementation of a new solution also has emotional and political implications, additional human resources beyond those directly involved in performing the implementation steps must be considered, and this is where acceptance planning is integrated into this stage of the implementation plan.

As decision makers finalize the convergent list of action steps in the previous implementation planning stage, they are very likely also asking what resources are needed to perform these implementation action steps. A divergent list of all kinds of physical resources needed for carrying out the previously defined action steps answers this basic question. The evaluation criteria to be used for this list of physical resources will focus on questions about the availability of the physical resources, their costs, what kinds of expertise (software, engineering, etc.) are needed, what kinds of control over acquiring and maintaining the resources needed; and in addition, decision makers will want to know whether the resources needed are scarce and without alternatives, whether these necessary and vital resources are of high quality (meet necessary standards), and whether they will be delivered on time. Because the previously determined action steps somewhat hamper (out of necessity) the divergent listing of physical resources in this stage and because the evaluation criteria introduce numerous preordained organizational and contextual-environmental boundaries and limitations on the final choices of physical resources, there is more emphasis on the convergent critical thinking framework element needed to address the choices of physical resources.

Tim Hurson has constructed a tool that can be used to identify and understand the physical resources required by an implementation plan, and by means of iterative use of the format described below a convergent list of such resources can be created. Hurson calls his tool the EFFECT tool; the letters stand for energy, funds, free time, expertise, conditions, and things. The tool's matrix structure is shown in figure 6.2.[9]

A switch to the divergent creative thinking framework element is necessary for dealing with the human resource side of this stage. There is a two-part agenda to be followed in the identification and choosing of human resources to be involved in the implementation of the chosen solution. First, it seems logical to identify the human resources

E	F	F	E	C	T
Energy	Funds	Free time	Expertise	Conditions	Things
What levels or types of energy are needed to complete each action step?	What financial resources are needed to complete each action step?	How much time is needed to complete each action step?	What type or level of knowledge is needed to complete each action step?	What conditions are needed to complete each action step?	What things, such as material resources or equipment, are needed to complete each action step?

Figure 6.2 EFFECT Technique for Identifying Physical Resources for Implementation Planning.

needed to perform the implementation action steps that have been determined.

Many people or categories of people who are to perform each action step should be listed in the divergent list of human resources. Tools for generating human resource lists are provided later in the description of this stage.

The obvious major reduction evaluation criteria will focus on assessing whether people have the skills and expertise needed to perform the new action steps. There will be other organizational and labor market considerations, such as cost and availability of competent labor, costs to train or retrain labor, and turnover and replacement costs.

The resultant convergent list of human resources necessary to perform the implementation action steps should now be established, and the tools to help do this will also be provided later. Now attention turns to examining the second part of the human resource side of implementation, which has often been called acceptance planning. This agenda represents a shift away from focusing on the people who will be asked to perform the implementation action steps to the people who hold power and influence over resources that may be needed to execute the implementation plan. The prior list of actions steps, physical resources, and human resources for performing the implementation action steps have been the main components of the plan thus far, and armed with this information, decision makers need to know whether powerful and influential people will support or resist the plan.

Any of these parties, among them solution users, implementers, recipients, and bystanders, can have positive or negative emotional reactions to a proposed new solution. Decision makers need to identify the specific key resisters and then develop strategies to turn them into key supporters if possible. The same specific identification process needs to be applied to key supportive stakeholders called assistors, who are defined as individuals, groups, or organizations that have a vested interest in the proposed solution; they are usually in positions with decision-making authority or are influential with respect to the success of the solution's implementation. These extreme players, on both sides, are the ones decision makers should pay attention to from a political viewpoint if they want to have all the resources necessary to complete the implementation plan successfully.

There are a number of tools or techniques that can be used to generate the divergent and convergent lists of human resources. As before, this analysis can begin with the starter questions such as these: "What human resources are available?" "Who are the solution implementers, users, recipients, and bystanders?" "Who is best equipped to carry out implementation step XXX?"

One tool for generating two broad lists of categories of people is called Assisters and Resisters; the categories consists of those willing to assist in implementing the proposed change and those resisting the proposed change. To organize the search for these people, the tool begins with using the "journalistic six" questions (also known as interrogatives or the 5 Ws/H questions): Who? What? Where? When? Why? And How? A generalized usage matrix format is shown in figure 6.3.[10]

A divergent tool that could help identify the strategic and influential people regarding the proposed implementation of the new solution is called Stakeholder Analysis; this tool can be used to identify prominent, strategic people who will support and those who will reject the proposed solution or change as well as to indicate what strategies might

Questions	Specific assistors	Specific resisters
Who What Where When Why How		

Figure 6.3 Typical Usage Format for Identifying Assistors and Resisters.

Stakeholder	Strongly resisting	Moderate resisting	Neutral	Moderate supporting	Strongly supporting	Movement strategy
AAA		X ——————→ T				
BBB			X ——→ T			
CCC		X ——————————————→ T				

Figure 6.4 Stakeholder Analysis of Three Stakeholders.

be used to change people's attitudes about the solution.[11] A simplified matrix format is shown in figure 6.4; X indicates where the stakeholder is now and T points to where decision makers would like to see the stakeholder in the future.

The last column in the above matrix labeled "movement strategy" is key to getting people to change their minds about an issue. Developing a strategy to gain more acceptance of the proposed solution can be attempted with the use of two techniques called bug list and role reversal. The bug list technique capitalizes on people's tendency to find fault with things around them. It is applied by asking the people in a group to identify things that irritate or "bug" them—in this case what bothers them about the potential solution or change. Each group member is asked to identify five to ten bugs, and then this big list is consolidated by voting. The group then brainstorms on ways to resolve the bugs, in this case ways to move the stakeholders toward acceptance.[12]

The role reversal technique involves putting yourself in the position of a person negatively reacting or simply resisting the proposed solution, anticipating that person's responses, and then coming up with strategies for responding to people's negative comments about the solution.[13] Using this technique and carrying out the recommended strategies should result in a much higher acceptance of the solution.

At this stage of the implementation process decision makers have lists indicating specific action steps and specific physical and human resources. How these elements will be combined is the subject of the next stage.

Implementation Plan: Stage 3—Aligning Resources

Tim Hurson has suggested that implementation alignment means that tasks (action steps), people, and resources all come together in a predictable time frame and people are held accountable for performing their responsibilities and using the resources.[14] In most models dealing with this stage of the implementation planning, the concern is on sequencing or scheduling, which essentially is the process of prioritizing only the action steps along a time line. The time line could range from immediate, short-term, intermediate, and long-term scheduling.[15] Specific ranges for each category must be clearly defined (does short term time mean 1 week, 1 month, or 36 hours?), and time windows for each action step noting the start and finish time that must be clearly defined.[16] Two other time-related aspects need to be assessed: first, an absolute deadline by which the implementation plan must be completely finished if it is going to be successful, and second, it is important to give specific consideration to the independent or dependent timing and completion relationships among the action steps.[17] Clearly, certain action steps must be done or started before other steps can be started, and other steps can run parallel. This clarification of the independent/dependent relationships also becomes a critical evaluation criterion to use for converging purposes. Establishing a time frame for the completion of each action step is at the heart of the implementation planning process and of this stage in particular.

Sequencing of action steps can begin in a divergent fashion by asking questions such as the following: "Which steps am I/we really going to take?" "Why, when, where, and how will those steps need to be taken?" "When will each step be completed?" "When will the step begin/end?"[18] Sequencing is only about spelling out what action steps are to happen when, and therefore it is only taking into account one part of the two parts needed for complete alignment to occur. The second part requires that people and resources be matched to individual action steps in a responsible and accountable way. If no one is held responsible or accountable for an action step, that step will not get done; an action step that is not done can have enormous negative consequences for the implementation plan's success. Being responsible for an action step means that individuals have accepted doing the work required for the step. Being accountable means people are aware of what work has to be done and when, and their engagement can be direct—that is, they act as the responsible party—or indirect—that is, they assign the work to another party. In the latter case, the people who are accountable may delegate the work along a chain of command (up or down the hierarchy) or to an entire team (cross-functional team, project team, etc.) and hold the other party responsible for the work. Nevertheless, those accepting accountability still must ensure that the action steps they are responsible for are completed.

Implementation Plan: Stage 4—Determine Plan Outcomes

The implementation plan will eventually have to be evaluated to see if it was successful in producing the solution it was intended for. A separate and independent monitoring control system for the implementation plan must be set up to provide feedback information as to whether or not the implementation plan was successful in getting the solution put into practice. However, setting up those systems is not part of this implementation planning stage. A number of action steps were generated in stage 1 for creating the plan. Their successful completion could be determined by assigning some observable, success metric(s) to each action step. This metric could include meeting a timing requirement, task responsibility assignment, budgetary limit, resource acquisition target, or any other final or milestone metrics that indicate that the specific and individual action step was completed.

The assumption for this final stage is that if every action step has observable, realistic, and useable measures for determining its completion as well as the quality of completion, and if all the action steps are then completed in a quality fashion, then the implementation plan can be deemed successful. Seeing that the implementation was successful does not mean that the solution itself was successful in achieving the new future state situational conditions. Solution success, as was indicated at the beginning of the chapter, is a different matter but related to the success of the implementation plan.

Overall Summary of Stages and Formatting Examples to Create an Implementation Plan

A summary of what decision makers have to do throughout the four stages of crafting the implementation plan and examples of what the final implementation plan might look like follow here.

For *Stage 1: Generate Action Steps*, the action or work-related tasks for the primary solution must be specifically identified.

For *Stage 2: Aggregate Resources*, all the physical and human resources needed to carry out each previously identified action step must be carefully and diligently identified. Acceptance planning (identifying the resisting and supporting human resources for the solution) also needs to be done in this stage.

In *Stage 3: Align Resources*, all the resources are formally and specifically matched with each action step. This stage imposes a formal relationship on all resources by requiring the use of these resources on a predictable time schedule and the assignment of a responsibility/accountability relationship between a human resource and an action step.

Resources, time schedules, action step relationships, and action steps themselves have all been brought together from stages 1 through 3. However, what will make each action step successful has not been officially and specifically declared.

In *Stage 4: Determine Plan Outcome*, decision makers formalize the determination of the success of each action step by identifying and assigning observable and measurable plan outcomes and/or milestone outcome metrics for each action step. If all the individual action steps have been successfully implemented, then it is assumed that the overall implementation plan has been successful. This has resulted in a formalized measurement system for each action step and these results will become useful in establishing an implementation monitoring system in the next part of this process step.

Implementation Plan Tools and Techniques

Much of this information can be converted into computerized charts and programs such as Gantt (time progression) charts, PERT (program evaluation and review technique), or CPM (critical path method) charts and other project management software programs designed for creating visual planning documents and tracking (monitoring) the implementation of a plan.[19] However, decision makers must not lose sight of the fact that the data to be entered into these programs come from developments thought up by people. Original thinking is the cornerstone of developing a new implementation plan because it will most likely contain new action steps, require use of new skills and expertise, and will be plugged into new time lines and schedules.

Two worksheets indicating different formats for presenting this information are presented below. The example to be illustrated in both worksheets is the previously mentioned solution of requiring all customers of the auto recycling operation to provide the VIN of their vehicle when ordering a part. The specific action step is checking whether the company's computer software can successfully identify the VIN of all vehicles. The first example is a generic worksheet used for just that action step.[20] If the implementation plan contained more action steps, then there would be separate worksheet pages like the one shown in figure 6.5 for each action step.

A second worksheet for the same previously mentioned action step is shown in figure 6.6, and this one calls for answers to the basic 5 W/H questions so that a plan for that implementation can be developed.[21] Obviously, many more sheets will be required if the number of action

Action sheet	Step #

Step
    Run diagnostics to check if software can locate
    VINs for any vehicle
	Person responsible
	John – Mgr. of IT

Dependent on completion of
    All ten company computers are running the vehicle
    VIN identification software
	Additional participants
	    All six sales counter peo-
	    ple and two assistant parts
	    managers

Start End Duration 6:30 am 7:30 am 1 hour – 6/15	Notes

Deliverables or evidence of completion
    100% successful location of 25 random vehicle
    VINs	

Assistors   Actions to improve support
    John-Mgr. of IT
    Sam-Asst. Parts Mgr.
    Sally-Asst. Parts Mgr.	

Resisters Actions to gain support	

Resources   Actions to acquire
    Ten company computers and VIN identification
    software plus sales counter personnel	

Figure 6.5 Single Formatted Action Worksheet Incorporating All Four Implementation Planning Stages.

steps is larger. Numerous iterations of the information in these sheets are required if sequencing is a requirement for placing the sheets in correct order.

Developing Implementation Control Systems

In *Stage 4: Determine Plan Outcomes* the need to develop an implementation monitoring system became clear. It would also be prudent to develop an implementation learning control system at the same time. This learning system could be a major section in the written portion of the implementation monitoring control system report.

Planning for implementation		
Action Have all ten company computers operational and running VIN software program **Measure of success** All computers are connected to the VIN program	Who Start Where Why How	John – Mgr. of IT 6:00 am Finish 6:30 am Company location Need software to locate vehicle VINs
Action Run VIN software program to check 25 random VINs **Measure of success** All 25 random VINs are located	Who Start Where Why How	John & six sales counter personnel 6:30 am Finish 7:30 am Company location Successful VIN locators needed to serve customers
Action (Next major action step would appear if previous action step was successful) **Measure of success**	Who Start Where Why How	Finish

Figure 6.6 Formatted Implementation Planning Worksheet Using 5W/H Questions.

As with any new solution, its implementation plan is subject to errors, confusion, deviations, and subsequent failure. Decision makers should understand that the responsibility for implementing a solution does not end in the "pre-implementation" planning phase. In this phase the plan has been developed, but it has not been put into practice yet. The fully developed implementation plan's monitoring control system should also take into account collecting and analyzing feedback information during the implementation of the plan (a "during-implementation" phase) as well as after the plan has been implemented in a "post-implementation phase" (after the entire plan has now been fully put into practice). Thus, a complete implementation plan monitoring control system should gather feedback information on all three phases, pre-, during-, and after- implementation. It should also perform all of the four formal following steps necessary to create a fully functional control system: (1) establish baseline standards, (2) assign observable measurement metrics to each standard, (3) compare actual performance to standards, and (4) take corrective action if necessary.

Fully functional monitoring control systems provide the feedback information that allows implementers and decision makers to learn from what is happening during the implementation as well as after it has been completed. Deeper inspection of the feedback information and continuing monitoring of the what is happening while the plan is carried out and after it has been completed can lead to improved understanding and learning about the specific errors, overlooked components, deviations, and any other consequential factors.

Two very serious negative consequences may need to be addressed by decision makers if negative feedback information continues to mount during the implementation process. One possibility is that the original implementation plan goes through a series of modifications, refinements, reorganizations, or reprioritization of action steps and/or resources and schedules. This would mean recalibrating the existing implementation plan. However, if the original plan cannot be salvaged and recalibrated, then a new plan must be created. This represents a renewal (the replacement of something old with something new). Backup implementation plans or a different plan with new monitoring and learning control systems will then have to be developed.

Before serious doubts are raised about the validity of the plan it would be useful to ask in what ways the plan might be improved. In fact, this might be one of the critical questions to be asked right after the original first draft of the pre-implementation plan is completed. This is also the major question that should be asked any time during and after the implementation. Applying the 5 Rs approach (reanalysis, redevelopment, refinement, re-sortment, and possible reprioritization) as part of the critical thinking process is also necessary.

For example, Couger presents a checklist for asking for ideas on how an implementation plan can be improved. Examples, formatted as questions, starting with the central question "Can the plan be improved?" include the following:[22]

- To make it more practical, workable?
- To make it more acceptable to me and others?
- To make it less costly?

- To make it more morally or legally acceptable?
- To increase its appeal?
- To mitigate problems it might cause?
- To salvage more if it should fail?
- To make it easier to implement?
- To lessen risks or results of failure?
- To make it more timely?
- To make it easier to test?

If the learning control system could be formatted as part of a monitoring system written report in response to questions that helped focus on learning-related answers, Harris poses the following series of questions to start this thinking process:[23]

- Was the solution fully and accurately implemented?
- Did the solution work as implemented?
- Were there unanticipated, undesirable consequences?
- Does the implementation plan need to be adjusted to have the solution be more successful?
- Do the solution and its implementation require additional activities?
- Should the solution and its implementation be replaced with another solution and its corresponding implementation plan?
- Has the challenge environment itself changed?

Many project management control systems have computerized monitoring reporting systems that clearly convey feedback information on conditions pre-, during-, and after- implementation of the solution. Gantt charts, critical path networks, and PERT programs all provide feedback information related to the implementation process.[24] Even a close inspection of the various worksheets presented in this chapter on the presentation of the implementation plan can offer some revealing monitoring and learning feedback information if they are updated regularly. Additional work needs to be put into developing and reporting post-implementation feedback information in most of these monitoring systems.

Summary of Overall Decision-Making Process

The messy current state situations in the first step of the overall decision-making process have drawn the attention of decision makers because of the accompanying anxiety, frustrations, discomfort, and failure to meet the needs of decision makers or their organization. These current state situational conditions need to be changed into an improved future state situation. In the second process step, the relevant challenges represented by positive or negative problems or opportunities triggering these messy current state and anticipated future state situational conditions are identified. With more in-depth thinking and analysis, the underlying causes of these challenges should have been identified.

Armed with the relevant information about challenges and their causes, the decision makers in the third process step address option ideas that might be used to reduce, eliminate, or neutralize the problem challenges and/or enhance, strengthen, or increase the opportunity challenges predominately for future state situations. These new option ideas were then made more realistic, feasible, and useful through more intense thinking about how to turn some of them into viable potential solutions in this step. Preliminary attention was also directed at identifying some tentative information about the transition journey for these potential solutions.

In the fourth step of the decision-making process decision makers decide on a solution set containing a primary solution and one or two backup solutions to achieve a new future state situation. In the fifth and final process step decision makers have to consider how to implement the primary solution so that the future state change will be successful. Partial monitoring and learning control systems for the primary solution and concerns about ways to sustain the new solution were required as part of the fourth process step. Full monitoring and learning control systems tied to the three types of implementation plans were developed in the final process step.

As discussed, the decision-making process has been streamlined in that the number of major process steps has been reduced from six or eight to five. But this streamlining may seem folly to the casual reader who sees the following: many of the process steps are split into two or more major interconnected activities or phases, and consequence and feedback looping effects analyses are required for each process step. Moreover, the process has been extended into developing various control systems for both the primary solution and its implementation plan. In addition, analysis of transition journey possibilities has been included in the third process step and culminated in the fifth step where that analysis was integrated into the implementation plan. The requirement to use the seven thinking elements framework to respond to many open-ended, provocative questions characterized all five steps of the decision-making process.

However, if there are reductions in mistakes, deviations, wasted resources, reduced resistance to needed change and greater acceptance of the change such that decisions are made for the betterment of the human condition rather than for individual, functional, or parochial interests, then all the extra thought-provoking requirements should produce better decision-making results. From an observational and anecdotal perspective, the evidence seems to support that the decision-making process of major decision makers in all walks of life has not produced outstanding results. Perhaps it is time for decision makers to be held more accountable for better decision making, and perhaps the decision-making process described here may offer that opportunity. However, the answer is best left to those decision makers who engage in this decision-making process and to those who are recipients of this process.

The Chapter's Thinking Completion Box

Even though we have come to the end of the steps needed to complete the overall decision-making process and an overall summary of the entire decision-making process was just presented, there are still some important aspects of this last process step that decision makers needs to pay attention to such as the following:

1. Have you as decision maker kept a detailed mental and physical engagement with the whole implementation planning process or have you delegated responsibility and accountability to other people?
2. You should know better than anyone else who the resisters and assistors are regarding the solution you are proposing and how to work with them strategically.
3. Successful implementation cannot be determined until information is fully collected and analyzed for the phases before, during, and after implementation. Are you one of the principal conduits through which this information flows?
4. Has your preliminary idea of the transition journey turned out to fit your implementation plans, and do you understand the difference between them?
5. Do you still apply the seven thinking elements framework and the three-phase thinking protocol of planning, evaluating, and controlling in this step?

Notes

1 New Thinking Directions in Decision Making

1. Gerald J. Puccio, Mary C. Murdock, and M. Mance (2007). *Creative Leadership: Skills that Drive Change*. Sage Publications, pp. 148–151. Tim Hurson (2008). *Think Better (Your Company's Future Depends on it…and so does Yours)*. McGraw-Hill, pp. 164–170. C. Grivas, and G. J. Puccio (2012). *The Innovative Team: Unleashing Creative Potential for Breakthrough Results*. Jossey-Bass, pp. 205–206.
2. Robert H. Vaughn (2007). *Decision Making and Problem Solving in Management*. 3rd ed. Crown Custom Publishing, pp. 18–19.
3. Robert A. Harris (2002). *Creative Problem Solving: A Step-by-Step Approach*. Pyrczak Publishing, pp. 83–89. Tim Hurson (2008). *Think Better (Your Company's Future Depends on It…and So Does Yours)*. McGraw-Hill, pp. 87–88. S. G. Isaksen, K. B. Dorval, and D. J. Treffinger (2011). *Creative Approaches to Problem Solving: A Framework for Innovation and Change*. 3rd ed. Sage, pp. 138–144. Gerald J. Puccio, Mary C. Murdock, and M. Mance (2007). *Creative Leadership: Skills that Drive Change*. Sage Publications, pp. 190–192.
4. S. G. Isaksen, K. B. Dorval, and D. J. Treffinger (2011). *Creative Approaches to Problem Solving: A Framework for Innovation and Change*. 3rd ed. Sage, pp. 37–39. Gerald J. Puccio, Mary C. Murdock, and M. Mance (2007). *Creative Leadership: Skills that Drive Change*. Sage Publications, pp. 42–43.
5. S. G. Isaksen, K. B. Dorval, and D. J. Treffinger (2011). *Creative Approaches to Problem Solving: A Framework for Innovation and Change*. 3rd ed. Sage, pp. 42–46. Gerald J. Puccio, Mary C. Murdock, and M. Mance (2007). *Creative Leadership: Skills that Drive Change*. Sage Publications, pp. 43–44.
6. Robert A. Harris (2002). *Creative Problem Solving: A Step-by-Step Approach*. Pyrczak Publishing, pp. 76–79.
7. T. R. Harvey, W. L. Bearley, and S. M. Corkrum (1999). *The Practical Decision Maker: A Handbook for Decision Making and Problem Solving in Organizations*. R. & L. Education, pp. 31–33.
8. J. Dooley (1999). *Problem Solving as a Double-Loop Learning System*. Adaptive Learning Design. D. L. Caruth, G. D. Caruth, and J. H. Humphries (2009). "Towards an Experiential Model of Problem Initiated Decision Making," *Journal of Management Research*, 9 (3): 123–132. W. R. Torbert (2000). "A Developmental Approach to Social Science: A Model for Analyzing Charles Alexander's Scientific Contributions," *Journal of Adult Development*, 7 (4): 255–267.

2 Current, Future, and Transition Journey Situational Analysis

1. William J. Altier (1999). *The Thinking Manager's Toolbox: Effective Process for Problem Solving and Decision Making*. Oxford University Press, pp. 29–32.
2. Tim Hurson (2008). *Think Better (Your Company's Future Depends on It . . and so Does Yours)*. McGraw-Hill, p. 105.
3. J. B. Harvey, R. M. Kanter, and A. E. Carlisle (1988). "The Abilene Paradox: The Management of Agreement." *Organizational Dynamics*, 17 (1): 17–43.
4. S. G. Isaksen, K. B. Dorval, and D. J. Treffinger (2011). *Creative Approaches to Problem Solving: A Framework for Innovation and Change*. 3rd ed. Sage, pp. 57–64. Gerald J. Puccio, Mary C. Murdock, and M. Mance (2007). *Creative Leadership: Skills That Drive Change*. Sage Publications, pp. 91–94.
5. Gerald J. Puccio, Mary C. Murdock, and M. Mance (2007). *Creative Leadership: Skills That Drive Change*. Sage Publications, pp. 91–94.
6. C. Grivas, and G. J. Puccio (2012). *The Innovative Team: Unleashing Creative Potential for Breakthrough Results*. Jossey-Bass, p. 3.
7. S. G. Isaksen, K. B. Dorval, and D. J. Treffinger (2011). *Creative Approaches to Problem Solving: A Framework for Innovation and Change*. 3rd ed. Sage, pp. 65–66.
8. Tony Proctor (2014). *Creative Problem Solving for Managers: Developing Skills for Decision Making and Innovation*. 2nd ed. Routledge, p. 99.
9. William J. Altier (1999). *The Thinking Manager's Toolbox: Effective Process for Problem Solving and Decision Making*. Oxford University Press, p. 29.
10. Tim Hurson (2008). *Think Better (Your Company's Future Depends on it…and so does Yours)*. McGraw-Hill, p. 106.
11. S. G. Isaksen, K. B. Dorval, and D. J. Treffinger (2011). *Creative Approaches to Problem Solving: A Framework for Innovation and Change*. 3rd ed. Sage, pp. 61–62.
12. S. G. Isaksen, K. B. Dorval, and D. J. Treffinger (2011). *Creative Approaches to Problem Solving: A Framework for Innovation and Change*. 3rd ed. Sage, pp. 165–167. Tim Hurson (2008). *Think Better (Your Company's Future Depends on it…and So Does Yours)*. McGraw-Hill, pp. 118–119.
13. S. G. Isaksen, K. B. Dorval, and D. J. Treffinger (2011). *Creative Approaches to Problem Solving: A Framework for Innovation and Change*. 3rd ed. Sage, p. 166.
14. Tim Hurson (2008). *Think Better (Your Company's Future Depends on It…and so Does Yours)*. McGraw-Hill, p. 118.
15. S. G. Isaksen, K. B. Dorval, and D. J. Treffinger (2011). *Creative Approaches to Problem Solving: A Framework for Innovation and Change*. 3rd ed. Sage, p. 166.
16. S. G. Isaksen, K. B. Dorval, and D. J. Treffinger (2011). *Creative Approaches to Problem Solving: A Framework for Innovation and Change*. 3rd ed. Sage, pp. 166–167.
17. T. Daniel Couger (1995). *Creative Problem Solving and Opportunity Finding*. Boyd & Fraser Publishing. Tony Proctor (2014). *Creative Problem Solving for Managers: Developing Skills for Decision Making and Innovation*. 2nd ed. Routledge.
18. T. Daniel Couger (1995). *Creative Problem Solving and Opportunity Finding*. Boyd & Fraser Publishing, pp. 214–218.
19. T. Daniel Couger (1995). *Creative Problem Solving and Opportunity Finding*. Boyd & Fraser Publishing, pp. 321–324.
20. S. G.Isaksen, K. B.Dorval, and D. J. Treffinger (2011). *Creative Approaches to Problem Solving: A Framework for Innovation and Change*. 3rd ed. Sage, pp. 76–78. Tony Proctor (2014). *Creative Problem Solving for Managers: Developing Skills for Decision Making and Innovation*. 2nd ed. Routledge, pp. 108–109.

21. Gerald J. Puccio, Mary C. Murdock, and M. Mance (2007). *Creative Leadership: Skills That Drive Change.* Sage Publications, pp. 97–98. Michael J. Hicks (2004). *Problem Solving and Decision Making: Hard, Soft and Creative Approaches.* 2nd ed. Thompson Publishing, p. 109. Tony Proctor (2014). *Creative Problem Solving for Managers: Developing Skills for Decision Making and Innovation.* 2nd ed. Routledge, p. 114.

22. S. G. Isaksen, K. B. Dorval, and D. J. Treffinger (2011). *Creative Approaches to Problem Solving: A Framework for Innovation and Change.* 3rd ed. Sage, pp. 78–80. Gerald J. Puccio, Mary C. Murdock, and M. Mance (2007). *Creative Leadership: Skills that Drive Change.* Sage Publications, pp. 99–101.

23. Gerald J. Puccio, Mary C. Murdock, and M. Mance (2007). *Creative Leadership: Skills that Drive Change.* Sage Publications, pp. 99–100.

24. Michael J. Hicks (2004). *Problem Solving and Decision Making: Hard, Soft and Creative Approaches.* 2nd ed. Thompson Publishing, pp. 69–70.

25. Gerald J. Puccio, Mary C. Murdock, and M. Mance (2007). *Creative Leadership: Skills that Drive Change.* Sage Publications, p. 91.

26. Gerald J. Puccio, Mary C. Murdock, and M. Mance (2007). *Creative Leadership: Skills that Drive Change.* Sage Publications, pp. 117–119.

27. A. B. VanGundy (1988). *Techniques of Structured Problem Solving.* Van Nostrand Reinhold.

28. T. Daniel Couger (1995). *Creative Problem Solving and Opportunity Finding.* Boyd & Fraser Publishing, p. 184.

29. T. Daniel Couger (1995). *Creative Problem Solving and Opportunity Finding.* Boyd and Fraser Publishing, p. 184.

30. Tony Proctor (2014). *Creative Problem Solving for Managers: Developing Skills for Decision Making and Innovation.* 2nd ed. Routledge, pp. 111–112. T. Daniel Couger (1995). *Creative Problem Solving and Opportunity Finding.* Boyd & Fraser Publishing Company, pp. 187–189.

31. C. Grivas, and G. J. Puccio (2012). *The Innovative Team: Unleashing Creative Potential for Breakthrough Results.* Jossey-Bass, pp. 112–117.

32. Tony Proctor (2014). *Creative Problem Solving for Managers: Developing Skills for Decision Making and Innovation.* 2nd ed. Routledge, pp. 110–111.

3   Challenge Framing and Causal Analysis

1. Robert A. Harris (2002). *Creative Problem Solving: A Step-by-Step Approach.* Pyrczak Publishing, p. 26. S. G. Isaksen, K. B. Dorval, and D. J. Treffinger (2011). *Creative Approaches to Problem Solving: A Framework for Innovation and Change.* 3rd ed. Sage, pp. 70–71. Gerald J. Puccio, Mary C. Murdock, and M. Mance (2007). *Creative Leadership: Skills that Drive Change.* Sage Publications, pp. 127–131.

2. T. Daniel Couger (1995). *Creative Problem Solving and Opportunity Finding.* Boyd & Fraser Publishing, pp. 75–76. S. G. Isaksen, K. B. Dorval, and D. J. Treffinger (2011). *Creative Approaches to Problem Solving: A Framework for Innovation and Change.* 3rd ed. Sage, p. 71. Gerald J. Puccio, Mary C. Murdock, and M. Mance (2007). *Creative Leadership: Skills That Drive Change.* Sage Publications, pp. 130–131.

3. John Adair (2010). *Decision Making and Problem Solving Strategies.* Kogan Page, p. 50.

4. Robert F. Mager, and Peter Pipe (1997). *Analyzing Performance Problems: Or You Really Oughta Wanna.* 3rd ed. Center for Effective Performance, pp. 2–3.

5. Tim Hurson (2008). *Think Better (Your Company's Future Depends on It...and so Does Yours).* McGraw-Hill, pp. 114–116. Gerald J. Puccio, Mary C. Murdock, and

M. Mance (2007). *Creative Leadership: Skills That Drive Change*. Sage Publications, pp. 128–129.

6. William J. Altier (1999). *The Thinking Manager's Toolbox: Effective Process for Problem Solving and Decision Making*. Oxford University Press, p. 28. Robert F. Mager and Peter Pipe (1997). *Analyzing Performance Problems: Or You Really Oughta Wanna*. 3rd ed. Center for Effective Performance. Tony Proctor (2014). *Creative Problem Solving for Managers: Developing Skills for Decision Making and Innovation*. 2nd ed. Routledge, p. 61.

7. William J. Altier (1999). *The Thinking Manager's Toolbox: Effective Process for Problem Solving and Decision Making*. Oxford University Press, p. 28. Tim Hurson (2008). *Think Better (Your Company's Future Depends on It…and so Does Yours)*. McGraw-Hill, pp. 130–134.

8. Tim Hurson (2008). *Think Better (Your Company's Future Depends on It…and so Does Yours)*. McGraw-Hill, pp. 104–107.

9. William J. Altier (1999). *The Thinking Manager's Toolbox: Effective Process for Problem Solving and Decision Making*. Oxford University Press, p. 102.

10. William J. Altier (1999). *The Thinking Manager's Toolbox: Effective Process for Problem Solving and Decision Making*. Oxford University Press, pp. 119–121.

11. S. G. Isaksen, K. B. Dorval, and D. J. Treffinger (2011). *Creative Approaches to Problem Solving: A Framework for Innovation and Change*. 3rd ed. Sage, pp. 71–75.

12. T. Daniel Couger (1995). *Creative Problem Solving and Opportunity Finding*. Boyd & Fraser Publishing, pp. 183–184.

13. William J. Altier (1999). *The Thinking Manager's Toolbox: Effective Process for Problem Solving and Decision Making*. Oxford University Press, p. 119.

14. T. Daniel Couger (1995). *Creative Problem Solving and Opportunity Finding*. Boyd & Fraser Publishing, pp. 187–189. Tony Proctor (2014). *Creative Problem Solving for Managers: Developing Skills for Decision Making and Innovation*. 2nd ed. Routledge, pp. 111–112.

15. T. Daniel Couger (1995). *Creative Problem Solving and Opportunity Finding*. Boyd & Fraser Publishing, pp. 185–187. Tony Proctor (2014). *Creative Problem Solving for Managers: Developing Skills for Decision Making and Innovation*. 2nd ed. Routledge, p. 113.

16. S. G. Isaksen, K. B. Dorval, and D. J. Treffinger (2011). *Creative Approaches to Problem Solving: A Framework for Innovation and Change*. 3rd ed. Sage, pp. 76–78. Tony Proctor (2014). *Creative Problem Solving for Managers: Developing Skills for Decision Making and Innovation*. 2nd ed. Routledge, pp. 108–109.

17. S. G. Isaksen, K. B. Dorval, and D. J. Treffinger (2011). *Creative Approaches to Problem Solving: A Framework for Innovation and Change*. 3rd ed. Sage, pp. 73–74.

18. Tony Proctor (2014). *Creative Problem Solving for Managers: Developing Skills for Decision Making and Innovation*. 2nd ed. Routledge, p. 108.

19. Tim Hurson (2008). *Think Better (Your Company's Future Depends on it…and so does Yours)*. McGraw-Hill, pp. 155–156.

20. Robert A. Harris (2002). *Creative Problem Solving: A Step-by-Step Approach*. Pyrczak Publishing, pp. 76–79.

21. B. Andersen (2007). *Business Process Improvement Toolbox*. 2nd ed. ASQ Quality Press, pp. 123–125.

22. B. Andersen (2007). *Business Process Improvement Toolbox,* 2nd ed. ASQ Quality Press, 125–127.

23. CAPT/Center for Advancement of Process Quality (2011). *Process Quality*. Prentice Hall, pp. 132–133. B. Andersen (2007). *Business Process Improvement Toolbox*. 2nd ed. ASQ Quality Press, pp. 148–151.

24. Robert A. Harris (2002). *Creative Problem Solving: A Step-by-Step Approach*. Pyrczak Publishing, pp. 31–33.

25. CAPT/Center for Advancement of Process Quality (2011*). Process Quality*. Prentice Hall, p. 101. Robert A. Harris (2002). *Creative Problem Solving: A Step-by-Step Approach*. Pyrczak Publishing, p. 33.

26. CAPT/Center for Advancement of Process Quality (2011). *Process Quality*. Prentice Hall, pp. 135–136.

27. CAPT/Center for Advancement of Process Quality (2011). *Process Quality*. Prentice Hall, p. 138. B. Andersen (2007). *Business Process Improvement Toolbox*. 2nd ed. ASQ Quality Press, pp. 142–145.

28. B. Andersen (2007). *Business Process Improvement Toolbox*. 2nd ed. ASQ Quality Press, pp. 132–133. Tony Proctor (2014). *Creative Problem Solving for Managers: Developing Skills for Decision Making and Innovation*. 2nd ed. Routledge, p. 114. S. J. Parnes (1981). *The Magic of Your Mind*. The Creative Education Foundation/ Bearly.

29. B. Andersen (2007). *Business Process Improvement Toolbox*. 2nd ed. ASQ Quality Press, p. 133. Gerald J. Puccio, Mary C. Murdock, and M. Mance (2007). *Creative Leadership: Skills That Drive Change*. Sage Publications, pp. 97–98.

30. B. Andersen (2007). *Business Process Improvement Toolbox*. 2nd ed. ASQ Quality Press, p. 132.

31. Robert A. Harris (2002). *Creative Problem Solving: A Step-by-Step Approach*. Pyrczak Publishing, p. 32.

32. Robert A. Harris (2002). *Creative Problem Solving: A Step-by-Step Approach*. Pyrczak Publishing, pp. 33–34.

4 Generating Solution Ideas

1. T. Daniel Couger (1995). *Creative Problem Solving and Opportunity Finding*. Boyd & Fraser Publishing, pp. 118–122. S. G. Isaksen, K. B. Dorval, and D. J. Treffinger (2011). *Creative Approaches to Problem Solving: A Framework for Innovation and Change* 3rd ed. Sage, pp. 37–39.

2. S. G. Isaksen, K. B. Dorval, and D. J. Treffinger (2011). *Creative Approaches to Problem Solving: A Framework for Innovation and Change*. 3rd ed. Sage, p. 89.

3. C. Grivas, and G. J. Puccio (2012). *The Innovative Team: Unleashing Creative Potential for Breakthrough Results*. Jossey-Bass, p. 6.

4. C. Grivas, and G. J. Puccio (2012). *The Innovative Team: Unleashing Creative Potential for Breakthrough Results*. Jossey-Bass, p. 6.

5. S. G. Isaksen, K. B. Dorval, and D. J. Treffinger (2011). *Creative Approaches to Problem Solving: A Framework for Innovation and Change*. 3rd ed. Sage, pp. 37–38.

6. T. Daniel Couger (1995). *Creative Problem Solving and Opportunity Finding*. Boyd & Fraser Publishing, pp. 178–195. Robert A. Harris (2002). *Creative Problem Solving: A Step-by-Step Approach*. Pyrczak Publishing, pp. 57–68. Michael J. Hicks (2004). *Problem Solving and Decision Making: Hard, Soft and Creative Approaches*. 2nd ed. Thompson Publishing, pp. 113–167. Tim Hurson (2008). *Think Better (Your Company's Future Depends on It . . . and so Does Yours)*. McGraw-Hill, pp. 161–174. S. G. Isaksen, K. B. Dorval, and D. J. Treffinger (2011). *Creative Approaches to Problem Solving: A Framework for Innovation and Change*. 3rd ed. Sage, pp. 83–107. Tony Proctor (2014). *Creative Problem Solving for Managers: Developing Skills for Decision Making and Innovation*. 2nd ed. Routledge, pp. 231–253. Gerald J. Puccio, Mary C. Murdock, and

M. Mance (2007). *Creative Leadership: Skills That Drive Change.* Sage Publications, pp. 139–168.

7. T. Daniel Couger (1995). *Creative Problem Solving and Opportunity Finding.* Boyd & Fraser Publishing, pp. 415–416, 439. S. G. Isaksen, K. B. Dorval, and D. J. Treffinger (2011). *Creative Approaches to Problem Solving: A Framework for Innovation and Change.* 3rd ed. Sage, pp. 102–104. Tony Proctor (2014). *Creative Problem Solving for Managers: Developing Skills for Decision Making and Innovation.* 2nd ed. Routledge, pp. 128–134.

8. T. Daniel Couger (1995). *Creative Problem Solving and Opportunity Finding.* Boyd & Fraser Publishing, pp. 251–252.

9. Tony Proctor (2014). *Creative Problem Solving for Managers: Developing Skills for Decision Making and Innovation.* 2nd ed. Routledge, pp. 184–185.

10. Michael J. Hicks (2004). *Problem Solving and Decision Making: Hard, Soft and Creative Approaches.* 2nd ed. Thompson Publishing, p. 141.

11. A. B. VanGundy (1988). *Techniques of Structured Problem Solving.* Van Nostrand Reinhold.

12. S. G. Isaksen, K. B. Dorval, and D. J. Treffinger (2011). *Creative Approaches to Problem Solving: A Framework for Innovation and Change.* 3rd ed. Sage, pp. 117–118.

13. Tim Hurson (2008). *Think Better (Your Company's Future Depends on It . . . and so Does Yours).* McGraw-Hill, p. 174. S. G. Isaksen, K. B. Dorval, and D. J. Treffinger (2011). *Creative Approaches to Problem Solving: A Framework for Innovation and Change.* 3rd ed. Sage, pp. 116–117. Gerald J. Puccio, Mary C. Murdock, and M. Mance (2007). *Creative Leadership: Skills that Drive Change.* Sage Publications, pp. 161–163.

14. C. Grivas, and G. J. Puccio (2012). *The Innovative Team: Unleashing Creative Potential for Breakthrough Results.* Jossey-Bass, pp. 153–162.

15. Tony Proctor (2014). *Creative Problem Solving for Managers: Developing Skills for Decision Making and Innovation.* 2nd ed. Routledge, p. 125.

16. S. G. Isaksen, K. B. Dorval, and D. J. Treffinger (2011). *Creative Approaches to Problem Solving: A Framework for Innovation and Change.* 3rd ed. Sage, p. 128.

17. C. Grivas, and D. J. Puccio (2012). *The Innovative Team: Unleashing Creative Potential for Breakthrough Results.* Jossey-Bass, pp. 216–217.

18. Tim Hurson (2008). *Think Better (Your Company's Future Depends on It . . . and so Does Yours).* McGraw-Hill, pp. 182–183.

19. S. G. Isaksen, K. B. Dorval, and D. J. Treffinger (2011). *Creative Approaches to Problem Solving: A Framework for Innovation and Change.* 3rd ed. Sage, pp. 43–44.

20. S. G. Isaksen, K. B. Dorval, and D. J. Treffinger (2011). *Creative Approaches to Problem Solving: A Framework for Innovation and Change.* 3rd ed. Sage, pp. 46–47.

21. Gerald J. Puccio, Mary C. Murdock, and M. Mance (2007). *Creative Leadership: Skills That Drive Change.* Sage Publications, pp. 166–167.

22. Tim Hurson (2008). *Think Better (Your Company's Future Depends on It . . . and so Does Yours).* McGraw-Hill, pp. 185–192.

23. Gerald J. Puccio, Mary C. Murdock, and M. Mance (2007). *Creative Leadership: Skills That Drive Change.* Sage Publications pp. 99–101.

24. Tim Hurson (2008). *Think Better (Your Company's Future Depends on it . . . . . . and so Does Yours).* McGraw-Hill, pp. 180–184.

25. T. R. Harvey, W. Bearley, and S. Corkrum (1999). *The Practical Decision Maker: A Handbook for Decision Making and Problem Solving in Organizations.* R. L. Education, pp. 59–63.

26. C. Grivas, and G. J. Puccio (2012). *The Innovative Team: Unleashing Creative Potential for Breakthrough Results.* Jossey-Bass, pp. 225–230.

27. Tim Hurson (2008). *Think Better (Your Company's Future Depends on It…and so Does Yours).* McGraw-Hill, pp. 182–183.

28. S. G. Isaksen, K. B. Dorval, and D. J. Treffinger (2011). *Creative Approaches to Problem Solving: A Framework for Innovation and Change.* 3rd ed. Sage, pp. 43–44.

5 Choosing a Solution Set

1. T. R. Harvey, W. Bearley, and S. Corkrum (1999). *The Practical Decision Maker: A Handbook for Decision Making and Problem Solving in Organizations.* R. L. Education, pp. 43–45. S. G. Isaksen, K. B. Dorval, and D. J. Treffinger (2011). *Creative Approaches to Problem Solving: A Framework for Innovation and Change.* 3rd ed. Sage, pp. 119–120.

2. John Adair (2010). *Decision Making and Problem Solving Strategies.* Kogan Page, pp. 18–24. T. Daniel Couger (1995). *Creative Problem Solving and Opportunity Finding.* Boyd & Fraser Publishing, pp. 118–122. *Harvard Business Essentials: Decision Making: 5 Steps to Better Results* (2006). Harvard Business School Press, pp. 46–51. S. G. Isaksen, K. B. Dorval, and D. J. Treffinger (2011). *Creative Approaches to Problem Solving: A Framework for Innovation and Change.* 3rd ed. Sage, p. 32. Robert F. Mager, and Peter Pipe (1997). *Analyzing Performance Problems: Or You Really Oughta Wanna.* 3rd ed. Center for Effective Performance, p. 5. Tony Proctor (2014). *Creative Problem Solving for Managers: Developing Skills for Decision Making and Innovation.* 2nd ed. Routledge, p. 38. Gerald J. Puccio, Mary C. Murdock, and M. Mance (2007). *Creative Leadership: Skills that Drive Change.* Sage, p. 36.

3. William J. Altier (1999). *The Thinking Manager's Toolbox: Effective Process for Problem Solving and Decision Making.* Oxford University Press, p. 44. Robert A. Harris (2002). *Creative Problem Solving: A Step-by-Step Approach.* Pyrczak Publishing. Tim Hurson (2008). *Think Better (Your Company's Future Depends on it…and so does Yours).* McGraw-Hill, pp. 180–184. C. H. Kepner, and B. B. Tregoe (1965). *The Rational Manager.* McGraw-Hill, pp. 122–123.

4. Robert A. Harris (2002). *Creative Problem Solving: A Step-by-Step Approach.* Pyrczak Publishing, pp. 47–49.

5. S. G. Isaksen, K. B. Dorval, and D. J. Treffinger (2011). *Creative Approaches to Problem Solving: A Framework for Innovation and Change.* 3rd ed. Sage, p. 120.

6. *Harvard Business Essentials: Decision Making: 5 Steps to Better Results* (2006). Harvard Business School Press, pp. 47–48.

7. Tony Proctor (2014). *Creative Problem Solving for Managers: Developing Skills for Decision Making and Innovation.* 2nd ed. Routledge, pp. 258–285.

8. Tony Proctor (2014). *Creative Problem Solving for Managers: Developing Skills for Decision Making and Innovation.* 2nd ed. Routledge, p. 262.

9. Tim Hurson (2008). *Think Better (Your Company's Future Depends on it…and so does Yours).* McGraw-Hill, pp. 180–184.

10. S. G. Isaksen, K. B. Dorval, and D. J. Treffinger (2011). *Creative Approaches to Problem Solving: A Framework for Innovation and Change.* 3rd ed. Sage, pp. 122–123. Gerald J. Puccio, Mary C. Murdock, and M. Mance (2007). *Creative Leadership: Skills that Drive Change.* Sage Publications, pp. 163–165.

11. Tim Hurson (2008). *Think Better (Your Company's Future Depends on it…and so does Yours).* McGraw-Hill, p. 181.

12. T. Daniel Couger (1995). *Creative Problem Solving and Opportunity Finding.* Boyd & Fraser Publishing, p. 275. Tony Proctor (2014). *Creative Problem Solving for Managers: Developing Skills for Decision Making and Innovation.* 2nd ed. Routledge, p. 260.

13. T. Daniel Couger (1995). *Creative Problem Solving and Opportunity Finding.* Boyd & Fraser Publishing, pp. 282–285.

14. Tony Proctor (2014). *Creative Problem Solving for Managers: Developing Skills for Decision Making and Innovation.* 2nd ed. Routledge, pp. 266–267.

15. *Harvard Business Essentials: Decision Making: 5 Steps to Better Results* (2006). Harvard Business School Press, pp. 51–52.

16. William J. Altier (1999). *The Thinking Manager's Toolbox: Effective Process for Problem Solving and Decision Making.* Oxford University Press, pp. 43–78. Michael J. Hicks (2004). *Problem Solving and Decision Making: Hard, Soft and Creative Approaches.* 2nd ed. Thompson Publishing, pp. 178–186.

17. *Harvard Business Essentials: Decision Making: 5 Steps to Better Results* (2006). Harvard Business School Press, pp. 49–51.

18. *Harvard Business Essentials: Decision Making: 5 Steps to Better Results* (2006). Harvard Business School Press, pp. 52–53. Tony Proctor (2014). *Creative Problem Solving for Managers: Developing Skills for Decision Making and Innovation.* 2nd ed. Routledge, p. 273.

19. *Harvard Business Essentials: Decision Making: 5 Steps to Better Results* (2006). Harvard Business School Press, pp. 54–56. Tony Proctor (2014). *Creative Problem Solving for Managers: Developing Skills for Decision Making and Innovation.* 2nd ed. Routledge.

20. Michael J. Hicks (2004). *Problem Solving and Decision Making: Hard, Soft and Creative Approaches.* 2nd ed. Thompson Publishing, pp. 175–176. S. G. Isaksen, K. B. Dorval, and D. J. Treffinger (2011). *Creative Approaches to Problem Solving: A Framework for Innovation and Change.* 3rd ed. Sage, pp. 121–122.

21. Tim Hurson (2008). *Think Better (Your Company's Future Depends on it . . . and so does Yours).* McGraw-Hill, pp. 217–232.

22. J. K. Pinto (2013). *Project Management: Achieving Competitive Advantage.* 3rd ed. Boston, MA: Pearson, pp. 158–160. Robert H. Vaughn (2007). *Decision Making and Problem Solving in Management.* 3rd ed. Crown Custom Publishing, pp. 18–22.

23. J. K. Pinto (2013). *Project Management: Achieving Competitive Advantage.* 3rd ed. Boston, MA: Pearson.

6 Implementation and Aftermath Planning

1. Tim Hurson (2008). *Think Better (Your Company's Future Depends on It . . . and so Does Yours).* McGraw-Hill, p. 199. William J. Altier (1999). *The Thinking Manager's Toolbox: Effective Process for Problem Solving and Decision Making.* Oxford University Press, pp. 79–88.

2. Gerald J. Puccio, Mary C. Murdock, and M. Mance (2007). *Creative Leadership: Skills That Drive Change.* Sage Publications, pp. 186–190.

3. William J. Altier (1999). *The Thinking Manager's Toolbox: Effective Process for Problem Solving and Decision Making.* Oxford University Press, p. 79. Tim Hurson (2008). *Think Better (Your Company's Future Depends on It . . . and so Does Yours).* McGraw-Hill, pp. 200–201.

4. S. G. Isaksen, K. B. Dorval, and D. J. Treffinger (2011). *Creative Approaches to Problem Solving: A Framework for Innovation and Change.* 3rd ed. Sage, pp. 34–35, 115, 128–146. Gerald J. Puccio, Mary C. Murdock, and M. Mance (2007). *Creative Leadership: Skills that Drive Change.* Sage Publications, pp. 178–179. Michael J. Hicks (2004). *Problem Solving and Decision Making: Hard, Soft and Creative Approaches.* 2nd ed. Thompson Publishing, pp. 194–195. Robert A. Harris (2002). *Creative Problem Solving: A Step-by-Step Approach.* Pyrczak Publishing, pp. 83–87. Tony Proctor

(2014). *Creative Problem Solving for Managers: Developing Skills for Decision Making and Innovation.* 2nd ed. Routledge, pp. 286–289. T. Daniel Couger (1995). *Creative Problem Solving and Opportunity Finding.* Boyd & Fraser Publishing, pp. 304–306, 310–315.

5. Gerald J. Puccio, Mary C. Murdock, and M. Mance (2007). *Creative Leadership: Skills that Drive Change.* Sage Publications, p. 137.

6. S. G. Isaksen, K. B. Dorval, and D. J. Treffinger (2011). *Creative Approaches to Problem Solving: A Framework for Innovation and Change.* 3rd ed. Sage, pp. 39–42. Gerald J. Puccio, Mary C. Murdock, and M. Mance (2007). *Creative Leadership: Skills that Drive Change.* Sage Publications, pp. 146–148.

7. Gerald J. Puccio, Mary C. Murdock, and M. Mance (2007). *Creative Leadership: Skills That Drive Change.* Sage Publications pp. 147–148.

8. Gerald J. Puccio, Mary C. Murdock, and M. Mance (2007). *Creative Leadership: Skills That Drive Change.* Sage Publications, pp. 99–100. Tim Hurson (2008). *Think Better (Your Company's Future Depends on it…and so Does Yours).* McGraw-Hill, pp. 201–202.

9. Tim Hurson (2008). *Think Better (Your Company's Future Depends on it…and so Does Yours).* McGraw-Hill, pp. 205–207.

10. S. G. Isaksen, K. B. Dorval, and D. J. Treffinger (2011). *Creative Approaches to Problem Solving: A Framework for Innovation and Change.* 3rd ed. Sage, pp. 134–136. Gerald J. Puccio, Mary C. Murdock, and M. Mance (2007). *Creative Leadership: Skills That Drive Change.* Sage Publications, pp. 178–179.

11. Gerald J. Puccio, Mary C. Murdock, and M. Mance (2007). *Creative Leadership: Skills That Drive Change.* Sage Publications, pp. 179–182.

12. T. Daniel Couger (1995). *Creative Problem Solving and Opportunity Finding.* Boyd & Fraser Publishing, pp. 216–220.

13. T. Daniel Couger (1995). *Creative Problem Solving and Opportunity Finding.* Boyd & Fraser Publishing, pp. 318–319.

14. Tim Hurson (2008). *Think Better (Your Company's Future Depends on It…and so Does Yours).* McGraw-Hill, p. 200.

15. Gerald J. Puccio, Mary C. Murdock, and M. Mance (2007). *Creative Leadership: Skills that Drive Change.* Sage Publications, pp. 194–196.

16. S. G. Isaksen, K. B. Dorval, and D. J. Treffinger (2011). *Creative Approaches to Problem Solving: A Framework for Innovation and Change.* 3rd ed. Sage, pp. 138–140. William J. Altier (1999). *The Thinking Manager's Toolbox: Effective Process for Problem Solving and Decision Making.* Oxford University Press, pp. 82–88.

17. William J. Altier (1999). *The Thinking Manager's Toolbox: Effective Process for Problem Solving and Decision Making.* Oxford University Press, p. 82.

18. S. G. Isaksen, K. B. Dorval, and D. J. Treffinger (2011). *Creative Approaches to Problem Solving: A Framework for Innovation and Change.* 3rd ed. Sage, pp. 138–144. Robert A. Harris (2002). *Creative Problem Solving: A Step-by-Step Approach.* Pyrczak Publishing, p. 87.

19. William J. Altier (1999). *The Thinking Manager's Toolbox: Effective Process for Problem Solving and Decision Making.* Oxford University Press, pp. 92–93.

20. Tim Hurson (2008). *Think Better (Your Company's Future Depends on It…and so Does Yours).* McGraw-Hill, p. 208.

21. S. G. Isaksen, K. B. Dorval, and D. J. Treffinger (2011). *Creative Approaches to Problem Solving: A Framework for Innovation and Change.* 3rd ed. Sage, p. 141.

22. T. Daniel Couger (1995). *Creative Problem Solving and Opportunity Finding.* Boyd & Fraser Publishing, p. 318.

23. Robert A. Harris (2002). *Creative Problem Solving: A Step-by-Step Approach.* Pyrczak Publishing, pp. 92–96.
24. William J. Altier (1999). *The Thinking Manager's Toolbox: Effective Process for Problem Solving and Decision Making.* Oxford University Press, pp. 88, 92–97. J. K. Pinto (2013). *Project Management: Achieving Competitive Advantage.* 3rd ed. Boston, MA: Pearson, pp. 285, 317–320, 352.

Bibliography

Adair, John. 2010. *Decision Making and Problem Solving Strategies*. London, UK: Kogan Page.

Altier, William J. 1999. *The Thinking Manager's Toolbox: Effective Process for Problem Solving and Decision Making*. New York, NY: Oxford University Press.

Andersen, B. 2007. *Business Process Improvement Toolbox*. 2nd ed. Milwaukee, WI: ASQ Quality Press.

CAPT/Center for Advancement of Process Quality. 2011. *Process Quality*. Upper Saddle River, NJ: Prentice Hall.

Caruth, D. L., G. D. Caruth, and J. H. Humphries. 2009. "Towards an Experiential Model of Problem Initiated Decision Making." *Journal of Management Research*, 9 (3): 123–32.

Couger, T. Daniel. 1995. *Creative Problem Solving and Opportunity Finding*. Danvers, MA: Boyd & Fraser Publishing.

Dooley, J. 1999. *Problem Solving as a Double-Loop Learning System*. Adaptive Learning Design, 1–58.

Grivas, C., and G. J. Puccio. 2012. *The Innovative Team: Unleashing Creative Potential for Breakthrough Results*. San Francisco, CA: Jossey-Bass.

Harris, Robert A. 2002. *Creative Problem Solving: A Step-by-Step Approach*. Los Angeles, CA: Pyrczak Publishing.

Harvard Business Essentials: Decision Making: 5 Steps to Better Results. 2006. Cambridge, MA: Harvard Business School Press.

Harvey, J. B. R. M. Kanter, and A. E. Carlisle (1988). "The Abilene Paradox: The Management of Agreement." *Organizational Dynamics*, 17 (1): 17–43.

Harvey, T. R., W. L. Bearley, and S. M. Corkrum. 1999. *The Practical Decision Maker: A Handbook for Decision Making and Problem Solving in Organizations*. Washington, DC: R. & L. Education.

Hicks, Michael J. 2004. *Problem Solving and Decision Making: Hard, Soft and Creative Approaches*. 2nd ed. London, UK: Thompson Publishing.

Hurson, Tim. 2008. *Think Better (Your Company's Future Depends on It ... and so Does Yours)*. New York, NY: McGraw-Hill.

Isaksen, S. G., K. B. Dorval, and D. J. Treffinger. 2011. *Creative Approaches to Problem Solving: A Framework for Innovation and Change*. 3rd ed. Thousand Oaks, CA: Sage.

Kepner, C. H., and B. B. Tregoe. 1965. *The Rational Manager*. New York, NY: McGraw-Hill.

Mager, Robert F., and Peter Pipe. 1997. *Analyzing Performance Problems: Or You Really Oughta Wanna*. 3rd ed. Atlanta, GA: Center for Effective Performance.

Parnes, S. J. 1981. *The Magic of Your Mind*. Scituate, MA: The Creative Education Foundation/Bearly Limited.

Pinto, J. K. 2013. *Project Management: Achieving Competitive Advantage.* 3rd ed. Boston, MA: Pearson.

Proctor, Tony. 2014. *Creative Problem Solving for Managers: Developing Skills for Decision Making and Innovation.* 2nd ed. New York, NY: Routledge.

Puccio, Gerald J., Mary C. Murdock, and M. Mance. 2007. *Creative Leadership: Skills That Drive Change.* Thousand Oaks, CA: Sage Publications.

Torbert, W. R. 2000. "A Developmental Approach to Social Science: A Model for Analyzing Charles Alexander's Scientific Contributions." *Journal of Adult Development,* 7 (4): 255–67.

VanGundy, A. B. 1988. *Techniques of Structured Problem Solving.* New York, NY: Van Nostrand Reinhold.

Vaughn, Robert H. 2007. *Decision Making and Problem Solving in Management: Tools and Techniques for Managers and Teams.* 3rd ed. Brunswick, OH: Crown Custom Publishing.

Index